WATERSIDE
In Warwick

Richard Shurey

COUNTRYSIDE BOOKS

NEWBURY, BERKSHIRE

Designed by Graham Whiteman
Cover illustration by Colin Doggett
Maps and photographs by the author

Produced through MRM Associates Ltd., Reading
Typeset by Techniset Typesetters, Newton-le-Willows
Printed by Woolnough Bookbinding Ltd., Irthlingborough

Contents

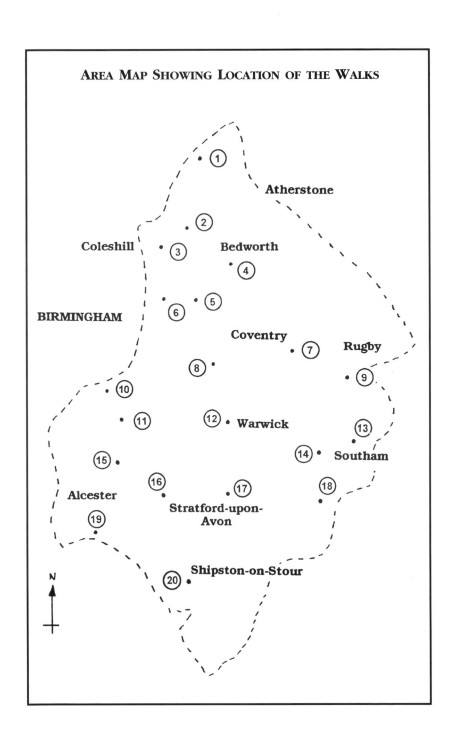

AREA MAP SHOWING LOCATION OF THE WALKS

Walk

PUBLISHER'S NOTE

We hope that you obtain considerable enjoyment from this book; great care has been taken in its preparation. Although at the time of publication all routes followed public rights of way or permitted paths, diversion orders can be made and permissions withdrawn.

We cannot of course be held responsible for such diversion orders and any inaccuracies in the text which result from these or any other changes to the routes nor any damage which might result from walkers trespassing on private property. We are anxious though that all details covering the walks are kept up to date and would therefore welcome information from readers which would be relevant to future editions.

INTRODUCTION

Warwickshire is as far away from the seas and oceans as it is possible to get in England; indeed, the very centre of the kingdom is the start of one of the walks in this book! However, the county contains a fine assortment of water. In Psalm 23 we are reminded of the Lord leading us 'beside the waters of comfort'. I always find inland waters have a wonderfully calming effect, so good for the soul in this increasingly hectic world.

The county is one of the great watersheds of England with the waters of some streams flowing into the Bristol Channel and others eastwards into the North Sea. There are famous rivers such as Shakespeare's Avon, twisting a way through delightful countryside. The feeder brooks and streams (surprisingly as Warwickshire has its fair share of industrial towns) are crystal clear and, bubbling over pebble beds, make a merry sound. There are canals too, which were the important arteries of commerce during the 19th century. In past days they carried the Midlands' coal and lime. Nowadays they provide the routes for holiday sailors to 'get away from it all'.

Then there are the reservoirs; many of these were constructed 200 years ago to provide water to top-up the canals. Today, besides affording opportunities for sport and fishing, they attract many species of birdlife and flora and are places of great beauty with invariably the bankside willows dipping low into the water. Other vast stretches of water provide drinking supplies. Draycote Water is almost 3 miles long and the water company has the enlightened policy of allowing access for lovers of quiet places.

Many large lakes have been formed as a direct result of industries which were abandoned years ago and which Mother Nature has swiftly reclaimed. In Warwickshire we find pools resulting from coal mining subsidence, the extraction of limestone for iron manufacture and from the incessant demand for sand and gravel to build roads and buildings.

All the different locations of water in the county can be enjoyed by walkers. Their beauty can be appreciated by everyone, but perhaps especially by those who find climbing hills rather too strenuous, as by the nature of the routes upland climbs are very rare. The paths can be muddy at some seasons of the year so wear stout shoes or boots. And don't forget the waterproofs – on the waterside walks more water may come down from the skies now and then! There are sketch maps to accompany each walk, and the relevant Ordnance Survey Landranger map is given so that you can follow the route in more detail if you wish. Directions on how to get there and suggestions for parking are also provided, but if you are parking by the roadside please consider other road users and those who live nearby.

For your greater enjoyment, pubs serving food, either on the route of the walk or near at hand for before or after the outing, are described and telephone numbers given so that you can check opening times etc., before you go. And you may like to make a day of it and visit some of the places of interest nearby, listed in a separate section after each walk.

I hope you enjoy your waterside walking in Warwickshire!

Richard Shurey

POLESWORTH AND THE RIVER ANKER

The Coventry Canal, which once carried coal from Pooley Hall Colliery, is now a tranquil companion through a changed landscape. The mines have long gone and grasses and trees cover the spoil heaps, passed on your way to a historic priory site.

A disused colliery rail bridge over the Coventry Canal.

There is a fine amalgam of waters on this walk. It starts from the large village of Polesworth where there is a wide bridge over the River Anker. In fact, the name of the place comes from 'Pol' meaning deep water. The towing path is squeezed between the river and the Coventry Canal. The waterway nudged many coalfields in the area so always commanded a steady trade and a local firm built the long, horse-drawn canal craft (some of them 72 feet in length) at Polesworth Docks. The canal took 22 years to construct, with 38 miles of waterway. The main coalfield at Pooley Hall closed in 1965 but the spoil heaps now clothed in green are a reminder of past days.

At the turning point of the walk at Alvecote are the few remains of a Benedictine priory. It was founded here in 1159 and attached to Great Malvern Priory. When the monasteries were dissolved it became a house, converted to a mansion in 1700. The only parts we can see today are the fine 14th-century gateway and a dovecote. The three-acre area has been grassed for family games and there are picnic tables and benches. Nearby is a nature reserve where there are lakes, teeming with birdlife, formed by land subsidence from the mining era.

There are several pubs in Polesworth (see the sketch map). If you are partial to spicy food you might like to try the Foster's Yard Hotel which specialises in Balti dishes. Parts of the hotel date from Tudor times with many rooms featuring the original cruck timbers and it is a Grade II listed building. There is an extensive menu which includes traditional English fare and a roast Sunday lunch. The Foster's Yard Hotel is open all day.

Telephone: 01827 899313.

- **HOW TO GET THERE:** Leave the M42 motorway at Junction 10. Take the A5 eastwards for just over a mile to Dordon. Turn left to Polesworth.
- **PARKING:** In the signed car park in Polesworth off Bridge Street.
- **LENGTH OF THE WALK:** 4 miles. Map: OS Landranger 140 Leicester and Coventry area (GR 262025).

THE WALK

1. From the car park turn left along Bridge Street. Cross over the B5000 to continue along Market Street. Go over the river to the canal. Gain the towing path and walk under the road. You now have the water on your left-hand side. Walk along the towing path now all the way to the priory. You will go under bridge 54 and the dilapidated bridge numbered 55, the motorway and the former rail coal bridge. At the next bridge leave the waterway. Gain the road and turn left over the canal to the picnic site and the ruins of Alvecote Priory.

2. When you have explored the site, retrace your steps over the canal and turn right through a metal barrier. Follow the bold path

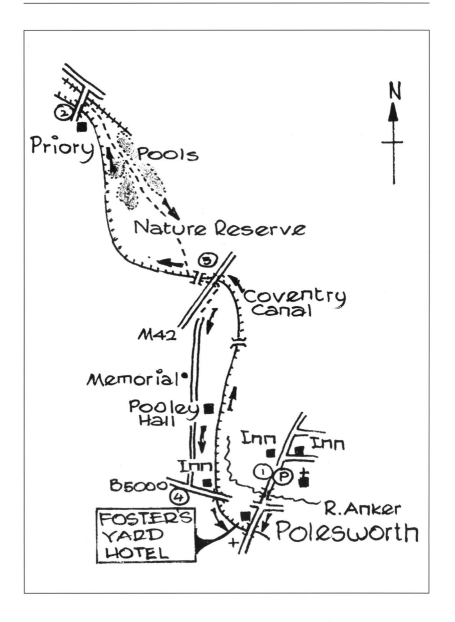

through the Nature Reserve. Amazingly, 190 species of birds have been recorded here. Go between pools and through a barrier. At a junction by a post numbered 7, keep ahead. Also maintain the direction within 150 yards at the next junction of paths to go

Pooley Hall

through another barrier of upright posts. Keep ahead along a very wide cinder track to regain the canal. On the left is a high heap of coal mine spoil where trees now grow. Walk along the towing path with the water now on the right.

3. Cross the water at the old rail bridge just before the motorway. Turn left and go under the motorway. The path is now along the old road and passes factories. Follow the vehicle way past a sadly rather unkempt war memorial ('to the undying memory...of those from the mine who fell in the Great War'). Pooley Hall overlooks the river and was built in 1507 by Thomas Cockayne, who was apparently killed by a neighbour on his way to church! Which is surprising as the Hall has in fact its own tiny chapel built by the authority of Pope Urban IV.

4. At the B5000 turn left to the canal bridge. Gain the towing path and retrace your steps to the starting bridge and Market Street.

PLACES OF INTEREST NEARBY
Along the A5 and the B585 the fascinating *Battle of Bosworth* site

The ruins of the Benedictine priory at Alvecote.

can be reached. Here on 22nd August 1485 was fought the decisive battle of the Wars of the Roses when Richard III was killed and Henry Tudor secured the throne. There is a self-guided Battle Trail (open daily) and a Visitor Centre which is open from 1st April to 31st October. Telephone: 01455 291040.

WALK 2

KINGSBURY'S LAKELAND

The pools of Kingsbury Water Park are not the only water features of this relaxing walk. A little-known canal and a revitalised river are also proof that man can repair the scars of industrial activity!

A restful spot in Kingsbury Water Park.

In the 1960s the Warwickshire County Council allowed worked-out gravel pits near Kingsbury to fill naturally with water with a view to establishing a water park. It was in 1968 that local authorities were given power by the Countryside Act to buy land for development into country parks and to their credit Warwickshire took speedy action to implement the new law. The first section of Kingsbury Water Park (about 156 acres) opened in 1975 and now over 600 acres are provided for an assortment of leisure activities. There are many miles of footpaths to discover the quiet places – and escape from the noise of the motorway which unfortunately also made use of the former derelict land!

The walk also includes a section along the towing path of the little-used Birmingham and Fazeley Canal. This waterway (authorised in 1784) was part of the Birmingham canal navigations which at their heyday in the middle of the 19th century were moving nine million tons of cargo each year. The river on the walk is the Tame, to which fish are now returning after a reduction in the level of pollution caused in the past by the vast amount of industry upstream.

There is a good selection of refreshment places on this walk. The Old Barn Coffee House by the car park serves a wide range of light refreshments with the salads especially tasty. Just off the route along the canal is the Dog and Doublet pub (telephone: 01827 872374) which was popular with the bargees in the days of commerce. If a slight diversion is made over the Tame and up the steps to Kingsbury there is a choice of several pubs. My favourite is the Royal Oak; it has only been an inn since conversion from the blacksmith's shop in 1920. Try the Royal Oak Grill here if you are hungry! Telephone: 01827 872339.

- **HOW TO GET THERE:** From junction 9 on the M42 go along the A4097 towards Kingsbury. Within 2 miles (at Marston roundabout) turn left towards Bodymoor Heath. The entrance to the Kingsbury Water Park is reached after a mile.
- **PARKING:** In the car park (fee paying) at the Water Park.
- **LENGTH OF THE WALK:** 4 miles (long walk) or 2 miles (short walk). Map: OS Landranger 139 Birmingham and surrounding area (GR 203958).

THE WALK

1. From the car park go to the road and turn right. Go over the motorway bridge to the canal bridge. Do not cross the waterway but turn right along the canal (the water is now on the left). Go past one lock. At the next lock leave the canal.

2. Walk to the right along the vehicle way at the far side of the house. Walk with Canal Pool on the left. There are about two dozen pools here, each providing for a different activity with angling and sailing being perhaps the most popular. At the far end of the next pool (Broomey Croft Pool) turn left (signed as being on the Heart of England Way). Go past toilets and the car park (on the right). At the end of the pool turn right to continue with Cliff Pool on your left. Cliff Pool is dedicated solely for wildlife so there is no public access

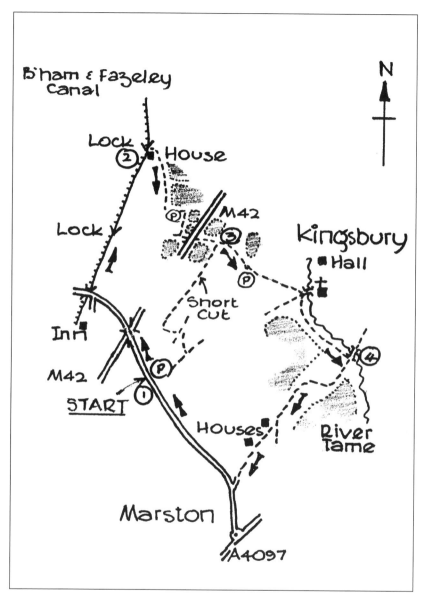

to the pool itself except to the bird hides to observe the wildfowl. Within 200 yards the way divides. Take the left-hand fork to go by Gibson's Pool. At a T-junction of tracks by Moorash Pool swing left to pass under the motorway.

3. At a junction it is decision time. For the shorter walk turn right – signed Visitor Centre and leading back to the car park. For the full walk keep ahead (signed Far Leys Car Park) to pass a pool with 'islands' of giant water lilies. A T-junction of tracks is reached. Turn left then at once right to walk over the grass, now heading towards the church tower. At a green with a football pitch walk along the right-hand edge, then walk over another football pitch to a hard path and a bridge over the river. Cross the hard path (not the river). The path now is never far from the left-hand River Tame. You will have noticed that overlooking the river plain of the Tame on high cliffs are two large buildings. The tower of Kingsbury church has been dominating the scene since the 14th century. To the left are the gaunt remnants of Kingsbury Hall; this was once a fortified manor house and perhaps was on the site of one of the royal palaces of the kings of Mercia. Today it looks far from its former splendour and needs urgent rescue.

4. At Hemlingford Bridge (a 'pensioned-off' road bridge) turn right along the vehicle way (once the main road). Keep ahead at a junction. Take care – when the way divides take the right-hand gravel way. Pass through a barrier by houses and continue along the old road to a junction at Marston. Turn right along the road back to the car park.

PLACES OF INTEREST NEARBY
Just off the route of the walk is *Broomey Croft Children's Farm.* Here is a good array of domestic and farm animals and birds – this is a 'hands on' farm which children love. Safe rides behind a tractor are given and there is a large playground and a cafe. Telephone: 01827 873844. More commercial is *Drayton Manor Park and Zoo* 3 miles north of Kingsbury. It was from 1790 the home of Sir Robert Peel (father of the Prime Minister who established the police force). The estate was sold in 1920 to become a large entertainment centre. There are fairground rides and a lot of noise and fun but this place really warrants a full day's visit. Telephone: 01827 287979.

A TRANQUIL WALK BY SHUSTOKE RESERVOIR

This amble around Shustoke reservoir, fed by the Little Bourne Brook, is a gentle relaxing stroll with no hills to negotiate. With an abundance of woods shielding the site it is difficult to appreciate how near you are to a bustling industrial region.

Shustoke reservoir was originally built to supply Birmingham with water. When the celebrated Elan Valley was dammed in 1905, Shustoke's water was given to the growing communities in Coventry and Nuneaton. The supplying Bourne Brook is only in a shallow valley so the building of the reservoir necessitated the construction of high banks. Today the Severn Trent Water Company have an enlightened policy of allowing the reservoir to be used for water-based sports such as sailing and angling and they are assisting in the exciting Forest of Arden initiative. This is to recreate the ancient woodlands which have been decimated after two centuries of industrialisation and development. Severn Trent's contribution is the ten year management plan to regenerate the woodlands on the north side of the reservoir with oak, willow, alder and pine trees. The first paths on the walk are alongside these woods. (The paths are not rights of way but permissive paths.) The reservoirs are a mecca for wildfowl and there are many seats and benches on the route to stop awhile to observe the birds. At the start of the ramble Severn Trent have created a fine picnic area.

The village of Shustoke (spelt Scotscote at the time of Domesday) was originally a mile away from the present site near the reservoirs. Today all that remains of the old settlement called Church End are the church, the former school, a row of almshouses and a farmstead or two. When the plague decimated the population in 1650 the surviving people moved to the present site, an attractive little village with a historic animal pound.

The Plough is a typical country inn which is friendly but not ostentatious and where ramblers are welcomed. The pies are an especial treat here after the ramble but I can also vouch for the 'toasties'. The place was once a farm labourer's cottage.
Telephone: 01675 481557.

- **HOW TO GET THERE:** Shustoke is on the B4114 Coleshill to Nuneaton road 3 miles east of Coleshill.
- **PARKING:** In the Severn Trent car park at the eastern edge of Shustoke.
- **LENGTH OF THE WALK:** 3 miles. Map: OS Landranger 139 Birmingham and surrounding area (GR 224910).

THE WALK

1. From the car park area cross the picnic site and climb steps to the path beside the reservoir. Continue along the bank of the reservoir with the water on the right-hand side. At the far end of the reservoir is a waymark post.

2. Turn left (signed Upper Reservoir). Go over a metal grid bridge to a fence by the Upper Reservoir. Turn left with the fence on your right side to cross the feeder brook. Reach a path by the railway, the Birmingham to Nuneaton line. Turn right to a junction of paths by a gate. Turn right (now on the Heart of England Way, a 100 mile long path from Cannock Chase to Bourton on the Water). Cross a bridge,

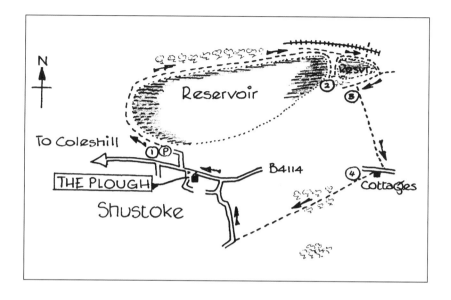

then there is a lovely path beside the feeder brook. Follow the path waymarks (not Circular Walk direction) to leave the brook. Within 30 yards climb a stile. Here there is a T-junction of paths. Turn right to border an arable field with woods on the right-hand side.

3. At a waymark post with a plethora of arrows turn left to keep at the side of the field. Follow the way at the borders of fields to a stile to a main road. Cross and turn right to walk alongside the cottages, which are adorned with colourful flowers in summertime. At the end take a signed path over a stile.

4. Follow the arrowed direction across the field passing by an electricity post. Continue to a stile to woods. The path is clear through the trees. Out of the trees maintain the heading alongside a right-hand hedge to a far corner stile to a farm track. This leads to a lane. Turn right. On the main road turn left to Shustoke. Go through the village past the Plough Inn on the little green. There used to be a typical village stores here in Shustoke too but sadly that has now gone. What does remain is the site of the village pound where stray animals were kept in the days before the enclosure act. Return to the car park entrance.

Shustoke reservoir.

PLACES OF INTEREST NEARBY

Seven miles south of Shustoke is *Meriden* which is reputed to be the centre of England. The spot is marked by an ancient market cross on the green. Over the centuries it has been a meeting place for political and social gatherings. At the opposite end of the green is the Cyclists National Memorial, a tall obelisk erected to the memory of cyclists who died in the two World Wars.

On the way to Meriden you will pass near the 14th-century *Maxstoke Castle* (not open to the public). It was here that Richard III rested before the fateful Battle of Bosworth and where Henry VII came after the victory that changed the history of the land. Maxstoke also has the ruins of a priory by a farmstead.

WALK 4

TOWPATH STEPS TO HARTSHILL COUNTRY PARK

The Coventry Canal, once a very busy commercial route, now sees only the occasional pleasure craft slip quietly by in the vale to disturb the swans and ducks. There is a nice contrast on this lovely walk with the upland and densely wooded Hartshill Country Park.

Above the woods at Hartshill.

The Coventry Canal is almost 40 miles in length and journeys through quite a level contour, so there are only 13 narrow beamed locks for the inland boatmen to negotiate. The canal was opened in 1790 after some 20 years of authorisation and construction. The plan was to join the Oxford Canal at Hawkesbury with the Trent and Mersey Canal so that London and the north could be linked for through traffic. This was one of the more profitable waterways as its staple cargo was coal from the Midland pits. It returned a dividend to the shareholders right up to nationalisation in the 20th century and although not the prettiest canal overall it is an important link with other waterways. The section covered on this walk is one of the most attractive parts and leads us to a splendid Country Park.

Hartshill Country Park covers almost 140 acres, most of it wooded with magnificent trees (some are remnants of the ancient Forest of Arden). The Park is on an island of rocks high above the plain and the canal and affords wide views to be enjoyed on the walk. The route passes through Hartshill Green. Rather bizarrely, the bus shelter is a monument to one of the great poets of the Midlands; Michael Drayton was born in the nearby Chapel Cottage in 1563. Sadly, the cottage was demolished in living memory. When Sir John Betjeman opened the monument he quoted from the poet:

> 'Clear had the day been from the dawn
> All chequered was the sky
> Thin clouds like scarfs of cobweb lawn
> Veiled heaven's most glorious eye.'

The inn is at Hartshill Green. The Stag and Pheasant is a workaday pub – no frills but an honest old-fashioned hostelry where the welcome to walkers is friendly. It was once the pub frequented by local miners and quarrymen – there are still quarries in the area but the mines have long gone. Traditional bar snacks are available and there are outside benches and tables for those sunny days. Telephone: 01203 393173.

- **HOW TO GET THERE:** From the A5 at Atherstone take the B4114, then follow the signs for Hartshill Country Park along the lanes to the car park.
- **PARKING:** At the Country Park car park.
- **LENGTH OF THE WALK:** $3^1/_2$ miles. Map: OS Landranger 140 Leicester and Coventry area (GR 320940).

THE WALK

1. From the car park and Visitor Centre of the Country Park take the path signed Hayes Wood. Go by a seat and through coppiced trees (which once supplied wood blocks for the manufacture of hats at Atherstone). At a bold T-junction turn left along a wide cinder way, then right by a post numbered 3. Drop downhill and go over a wooden bridge and keep ahead. Also keep ahead at post number 4

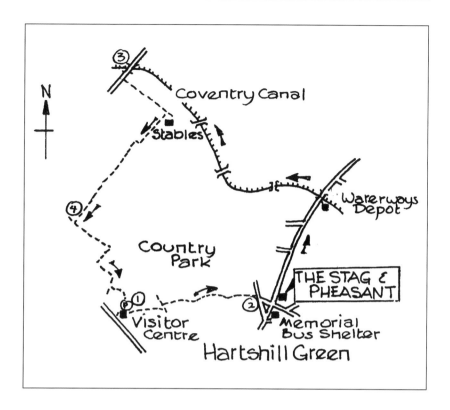

and at a crossroads of tracks. Remain on the main path to descend to a raised causeway. Climb the steps (and enjoy the lovely view) to emerge on a road by garages.

2. Turn right, then left on Atherstone Road at Hartshill Green. Look out for the Michael Drayton memorial bus shelter. Pass the Stag and Pheasant pub on your way towards the canal. Drop down to the canal bridge, which you cross. Gain the towing path then go under the road. Continue beside the canal with the water on your left. At the bridge numbered 36 (on the far side) leave the canal.

3. Climb to the lane and turn left over the water. Within 100 yards take a signed path along a vehicle way, left. Just before a stable block take the path signed to the right, then at once left to continue alongside a right-hand hedge. On the hilltop climb a stile to a clear track. Turn left.

The bus shelter erected in memory of the Midlands poet, Michael Drayton.

4. Drop down the valley then turn 90 degrees left alongside a wire fence. After ¼ mile go through a hedge gap then regain the old heading now with a hedge on the left. Follow the border of the field around a corner to enter woods. Within a few steps there is a junction of tracks by a post numbered 5. Take the right-hand fork along a clinker path which climbs uphill. Go by a seat. A few yards further climb steps on the right. At a meeting of paths bear right (arrowed blue) to continue uphill to border St Lawrence's Wood.

By post number 8 swing left to walk along a track through rough pasture. Keep on the bold path which soon resumes the uphill climb alongside woods on the left-hand side. The path soon enters the woods – stay on the main path to the car park.

PLACES OF INTEREST NEARBY

This is *George Eliot* country and there are many reminders of the great author at nearby Nuneaton and in the surrounding area. She was born on the estate of Arbury Hall (the hall is said to be one of the finest 18th-century Gothic mansions in the country). *The Mill on the Floss* was based on a mill near Nuneaton. Nuneaton is no Stratford-upon-Avon but the town is rightly proud of Mary Ann Evans (George Eliot's real name) and has named many buildings and a park after her.

WALK 5

PLEASANT POOLS
AT MERIDEN

Two pools, home to many species of wildfowl, are the watery highlights of this pleasant walk, which begins at the very heart of England on the village green at Meriden.

Looking across the fields to Birmingham.

At the beginning of this route, the path runs near a delightful mere and village pool where many species of duck have set up home. In this peaceful place it is difficult to appreciate that an international airport is only a mile or so distant. Then soon you overlook a large lake formed when sand and gravel was extracted. Like other such lakes the wildfowl soon came and set up home and there is now a fascinating quarryside walk where the antics of the birds can be studied. (Sadly the area is still being worked for minerals so there will also probably be the clatter of machinery!)

The walk starts at Meriden – a name which comes from the Old

25

English 'myrge-denu' or pleasant valley. It is said that the very centre of England is at the market cross on the village green but just how this is determined with our indented coastline remains a mystery! In the great coaching age this was a very important place with seven inns in the village providing rest and accommodation and three blacksmiths to care for the horses. The church is $1/2$ mile from the village. Dedicated to St Lawrence, it was built on the instructions of the notorious Lady Godiva, who was the wife of Earl Leofric of Coventry. The church (which has much fine Norman work) became isolated at the time of the Great Plague when villagers moved away for safety's sake. Not far away is the old St Lawrence's Well in which the first Christians of the parish were baptised.

There are two pubs to choose from in Meriden. One (with its sensible floors and much used by walkers) is the Queen's Head at the east end of the village. This is a survivor from the era of stage coaches and survived again when the village was by-passed taking away much of the passing trade. It is now a popular hostelry offering good food and drink. The traditional ploughman's is excellent value and there are 'Tiddler' portions for children. Telephone: 01676 522256. The other pub, the Bull's Head, which is passed on the walk, was another coaching inn; it is rather more 'up-market' but still is a welcoming hostelry. Princess Victoria is said to have stopped here in 1832. An especially attractive feature is the outside patio – full of plants and hanging greenery where one can take one's food and drink. I loved the Marinated Chicken and Raspberry Salad.

Telephone: 01676 523798.

- **HOW TO GET THERE:** From Birmingham go along the A45 then (past the Stonebridge junction) bear right along the B4102 to Meriden.
- **PARKING:** Quiet streetside parking off the main road.
- **LENGTH OF THE WALK:** $4^1/2$ miles (or 2 miles for the shorter walk). Map: OS Landranger 139 Birmingham and surrounding area (GR 239820).

THE WALK

1. From the village cross on the green (the centre of England, so they say) go past the tall cyclists' memorial. This was put up between the wars and now commemorates cyclists who died in the

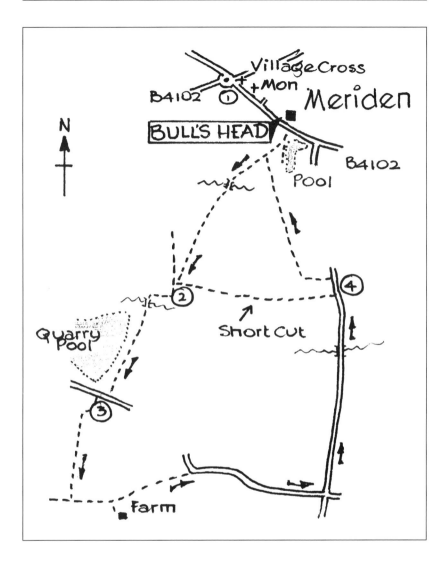

two World Wars; an annual service of remembrance is held here each May. Opposite the Bull's Head turn right along the drive of Meriden Hall. Within a few steps the path leaves the drive off to the right. The fenced way goes to a stile to a pasture. Here three paths are signed. Take the middle path. Cut across the pasture, passing by an isolated tree to go over a bridge and stile about 100 yards to the left of the far diagonal corner. Cut off the corner of the next field to climb a stile. Follow the arrowed direction, passing a bush to continue to a distant corner.

2. For the shorter walk, take the way signed sharp left and follow the path through the fields on a constant direction to a road. Turn left up the road and rejoin the walking directions at 4 below.

For the longer walk, climb the stile and turn left. Walk along a fenced way then turn right through a copse and alongside a left-hand brook. After 200 yards the path turns sharp left to cross the brook over a wide bridge. Follow the path alongside the quarry pool to a stile to a lane. Turn right, then left over a stile by a metal gate.

3. Continue along the path alongside left-hand woods. The path then twists right, then left by a diversion sign. Follow the fieldside path to a farm road. Turn left to a junction and keep ahead along the road. Turn left at a crossroads. After 1/2 mile we join the shorter route.

4. Just beyond, turn left off the road up steps and over a rather concealed stile. Follow the arrowed way over the brow of the rise to climb a stile under an old chestnut tree. Enjoy the fine view now with the towers of Birmingham and the NEC buildings on a far horizon. Bear right to another stile and follow the arrowed direction to drop downhill. Climb a stile by a metal gate. Keep ahead to join the outward route and retrace your steps to the green at Meriden.

PLACES OF INTEREST NEARBY

Birmingham International Airport is a few miles to the west and well worth a visit. There is a wide assortment of planes coming and going which can be seen from the Spectator's Viewing Area. Nearby is the famous *National Exhibition Centre* – there may well be an exhibition like the Motor or Spring Show to visit when in the area.

THE MERRY RIVER BLYTHE

The Blythe is a gentle meandering river that makes an unhurried journey through willow-fringed banks before joining the Tame. This walk also takes you past a deep pool rich in birdlife and over a bridge at Hampton in Arden which once echoed to the clatter of the long trains of packhorses that plied the old salt route from Droitwich.

Footbridge over the River Blythe.

The soils around Hampton in Arden are very gravelly; although this was an asset in past days and provided employment, when the quarrying finished the huge pit left behind was something of a blot on the landscape. However, the water-filled pit has now been pleasantly landscaped, the old quarry buildings have gone and wildfowl have made their home here. It is a pleasure to walk the grassy tracks around the fringes of the pool. The River Blythe twists a snake-like route to the east of the willow-fringed expanse of water. The name comes from the Old English 'blipe' and means 'gentle' or 'merry' – so appropriate when you see the water rippling over the pebbles. Towards the end of the walk the river flows under an ancient packhorse bridge. Here the current has been wearing away the cutwaters since the 1500s, on a crossing on the route of the salt way from Droitwich to Coventry and beyond. There are five arches on the bridge and on one pier are the remains of an old cross; no doubt it was here that travellers prayed for a safe passage through the forest.

Arden Forest was vast in those days and one record claimed that a squirrel could leap from tree to tree from one side to the other without touching the ground. Shakespeare loved Arden – it is said that he who knows Arden has looked into the heart of England and the Forester of Arden in *As You Like It* reminds us that 'this life is so jolly'. Hampton in Arden has a fine church that was built in 1130 and we can still see Norman work. Even earlier on the site was a Saxon place of worship. The sturdy tower was once topped by a landmark spire but it tumbled down in 1643 when struck by lightning. Perhaps Hampton's most celebrated resident was Sir Frederick Peel, the son of the 19th century Prime Minister Sir Robert Peel (who started the modern police force). Sir Robert built the Manor House for his son Frederick, who was a railway commissioner. Not surprisingly, Frederick insisted that a station was built in his village although the population then was modest.

There are two pubs in Hampton, at either end of the High Street. The most convenient for this walk is the Mitchells and Butler's White Lion, which is perhaps the inn mentioned in the Domesday Survey of 1086 as being opposite the church. Records have certainly established that there has been a hostelry here for 400 years. The place has been sympathetically modernised and the food is first class with much home-made fare. The steaks are just right for hungry ramblers, youngsters have a tempting separate menu, and there are outdoor benches and tables. There are the favourite Midland beers such as Brew XI and Bass and also guest beers.

Telephone: 01675 442833.

- **HOW TO GET THERE:** Hampton in Arden is south-east of Birmingham on the B4102 midway between Solihull and Meriden.
- **PARKING:** Street-side parking off the main road.
- **LENGTH OF THE WALK:** 5 miles. Map: OS Landranger 139 Birmingham and surrounding area (GR 203807).

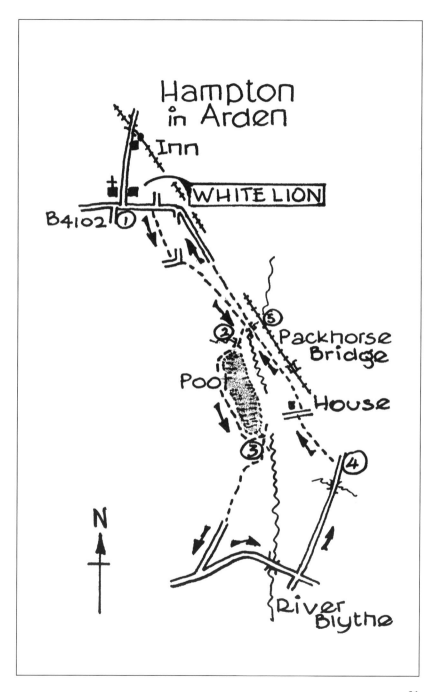

The Walk

1. Opposite the church walk down Marsh Lane. After about 400 yards take a signed path over a stile on the right. In the meadow continue to the very far left-hand corner. Climb a stile then walk to a second stile to a road. Turn left. As the road bends sharp left, keep ahead. The path is signed along a house drive, then beside the house and garden to a field. Keep the heading to a stile. There are now further stiles as the path through the fields gradually nears the railway on the left.

2. After a stile the path goes through bushes to a junction of paths near a vehicle way. Do not go through the barrier to the vehicle way but take a track to the right. This passes a pool (on the left) where yellow water lilies bloom. Follow the clear path which crosses a brook – a tributary to the River Blythe.

A large pool is reached. Turn right then left. Walk with the large pool on your left.

3. At the far end bear left to a T-junction. Turn right and go past a building on the right. Keep ahead at a junction of ways. Go by a left-hand wood and the river and around bends to a lane. The lane goes to a road. Turn left to cross the river. At a crossroads turn left along Bradnock's Marsh Lane. Go past one signed path. At the next on the left (beside a concrete farm drive) climb the stile to a pasture.

4. Take the arrowed direction then walk beside the hedge to climb a corner stile. Keep ahead to climb another by barns. Keeping to the left of the barns, maintain the direction to a lane. Continue right, then at once left. Climb another stile immediately then follow the path beside the left-hand border to a corner stile by a metal gate. Keep ahead to another corner stile. Over this turn right towards the railway. Turn left in the corner then follow the side of the embankment to a lane. (To the left is a house attached to the stump of a windmill tower.) Keep ahead to the end of the lane and pass through the barriers.

5. Follow the path along the raised causeway to cross the river over the packhorse bridge. Another raised causeway leads to a lane. This is Marsh Lane and leads back to Hampton in Arden.

A packhorse bridge over the river.

PLACES OF INTEREST NEARBY

Three miles south-east of Hampton in Arden is the interesting village of *Berkswell*. The well goes back to Saxon times and it was here that the local monks were baptised. On the green are ancient stocks; perhaps the five holes were to accommodate a one-legged offender with his colleagues in crime! Nearby is a little museum of country artefacts.

MARTHA IN RYTON POOLS

From the pretty little village of Bubbenhall, the route takes you past the very new and beautifully landscaped Ryton Pools and into some of the oldest woodland in Warwickshire – and don't forget to see Martha the Methane Bubble!

The peaceful Ryton Pools.

Some decades ago cattle grazed over these lands not many miles from Coventry. Beneath the fields were vast and valuable deposits of sand and gravel and there was an insatiable demand for these minerals with roads and buildings to be constructed. When the deposits were exhausted there were left large tracts of deep quarries and scarred earth. There was now a need for landfill sites for depositing the rubbish of the conurbations; Ryton being close at hand was the easy answer and for many years the lorries came day and night to fill in the quarries. When the area could take no more and when two million tons of rubbish had been deposited, imaginative folks could see that the former derelict eyesore would make an ideal country park. After five years of dedicated work the Chairman of the County Council opened Ryton Pools Country Park in 1996. The work of restoration involved covering the area with clay and top soil, then planting 2,500 trees and shrubs. Many lakes were retained or restyled and soon wildfowl and other wildlife, such as dragonflies, discovered this new habitat. The result is a popular country park which attracts walkers and families from near and far.

But where does Martha come in? It was found that the decaying rubbish was producing a large amount of methane gas which was going to waste. It was decided to build an electrical power station within the Country Park and so Martha the Methane Bubble was born! On this walk the little power station can be visited. There is a very informative exhibition, where the full history of the imaginative scheme to produce enough power to supply over 2,000 homes can be discovered. The route also goes through one of the oldest woods in Warwickshire – Ryton Wood. It was here at the time of Domesday (1086) and has a great assortment of coniferous and deciduous trees including many huge oaks. The woodlands are administered by the Warwickshire Wildlife Trust. (Please note that dogs are not encouraged.)

There are two pubs in Bubbenhall village, a pretty place nudging the River Avon with timber-framed houses and barns. Both are good places for refreshments. The Three Horse Shoes is off the route but you pass by the Malt Shovel. This building is over 400 years old and was once the court house where local felons were tried. The menu is extensive and all the fare is home-made. Italian dishes are a speciality with a great variety of pasta. There will always be a vegetarian dish or two and children have a great selection of 'with chips' favourites. Normal pub opening hours apply.

Telephone: 02476 301141.

- **HOW TO GET THERE:** Bubbenhall is just off the A445, 5 miles south of Coventry.
- **PARKING:** On quiet roadsides in the village or by the playing field which is passed early on the route.
- **LENGTH OF THE WALK:** $3^1/_2$ miles. Map: OS Landranger 140 Leicester and Coventry (GR 360726).

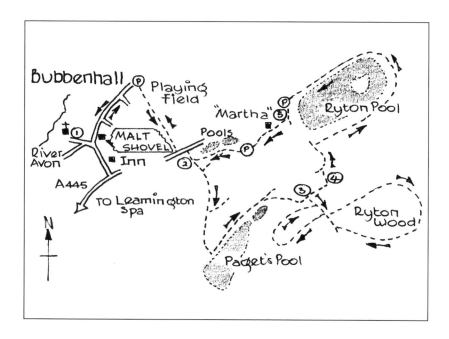

THE WALK

1. From the church, which dates from the 13th century and has a fine stone tower, walk along Church Road. Turn left, then at once left again down Lower End to pass the Malt Shovel Inn. The lane is signed as a no through road. Go past junctions to the very end. Turn right so a car park and playing field are on the left-hand side.

Climb a stile to a large pasture. Continue alongside the right-hand border to climb a stile to the main road. Cross and turn left. Within a few steps turn right through a gate to the Ryton Pools Country Park. Follow the winding path. When the way divides take the right-hand fork.

2. The wide path runs near the border of the park. Keep ahead at junctions; the path leads to Paget's Pool. This is one of the most important sites in the county for dragonflies and it is said 14 species breed on the pool. There is a hide to observe the wildlife. When the way divides past the main pool take the wide track (signed Ryton Wood Trail) which climbs to the right. At the top turn right to enter Ryton Woods through a little gate.

3. Follow the clear waymarks in the wood; these lead you on a figure-of-eight route on lovely pathways of a little over a mile. Leave the ancient woods through the same little gate. Turn right to walk near a right-hand wire fence for 200 yards. By a vent drop down the bank left to rejoin the main track.

4. Turn right, passing through a barrier. Just before Ryton Water is reached take a path right. This climbs with the lovely pool where swans glide on the left. Follow the edge of the pool (which you always keep on the left). The path runs alongside the road. Near a car park go left alongside a left-hand wire fence which edges the water. After 50 yards swing right to climb steps. Follow the path with a large grassed area on the left.

5. Go by (though a visit is well worth while) the Martha complex and continue to the main car park and visitor centre. Take the path signed to the Bubbenhall Stroll. When the track divides after 300 yards take the right-hand (lower) way to pass right-hand pools. At a junction rejoin the outward path and retrace your steps to Bubbenhall village.

PLACES OF INTEREST NEARBY
The *City of Coventry* is 5 miles distant. Here is the shell of the cathedral which was bombed and gutted during the raids of the Second World War; the soaring 15th-century spire was saved to remain one of the best examples of the Perpendicular period in the country. Alongside is the splendid new cathedral designed by Sir Basil Spence which incorporated the best in modern building styles and art of the mid-20th century. Nearby is a statue by Reid Dick of Coventry's most famous character – Lady Godiva. The city has a good selection of shops.

THE TWIN WATERWAYS AT LOWSONFORD

The lovely Stratford-upon-Avon and Grand Union canals are the twin waterways of this walk, with plenty to see along these increasingly popular leisure routes including a fine church and an unusual lock-keeper's cottage.

The canal bridge by the Tom o' the Wood pub.

The Grand Union and Stratford Canals gradually nudge together to meet at Kingswood. This became a profitable place during the Canal Age as the Warwick and Birmingham Canal Company extracted the price of a lock of water for every boat which passed over the junction. The Grand Union Canal was only formed in 1929 when many companies were amalgamated. Before that the bargees had to negotiate rates on each individual section for a journey to London. Near Rowington the waterway goes through a long and deep cutting; one can hardly appreciate the huge amount of soil which had to be excavated. The Stratford-upon-Avon Canal was completed in 1816 and carried mainly limestone northwards and coal from the Midland fields in the other direction. Today it is one of the most popular leisure routes in the country, although the 56 locks on the 25 miles make it seem anything but a holiday!

The walk starts at Lowsonford. This was Lonesomford in old records ... 'a name, without doubt, derived from the former solitary character of the country where the ford crossed the little brook'. One can imagine the impact that the arrival of the new waterway made when it was completed almost 200 years ago. The railway was to follow, although it took over 35 years to finally complete when the original company withdrew after starting the branch line. There was talk of opening a station at Lowsonford but the First World War put a stop to both the station and the railway. The rails were removed to be used in France – but the ship was sunk in the Channel!

There are two excellent pubs, both of which are open all day and have extensive gardens at the water's edge. The Fleur de Lys near the start at Lowsonford (a Laurel pub) dates from the 17th century although it was once a terrace of cottages. The specialities are the Fleur de Lys pies which were first made way back in the 1950s when pub food was little more than a packet of salted crisps. The beers available include Flowers Original and IPA and a guest. Telephone: 01564 782431.

The Tom o' the Wood near Rowington was once the Old New Inn but it was renamed after Tom – a customer who owned a local sawmill. The popular pub has a very wide menu but ramblers often opt for the large mixed grill. Beers include Boddingtons, Flowers and Morlands. Telephone: 01564 782252.

- **HOW TO GET THERE:** From Henley-in-Arden take the A4189 and within 2 miles take a lane left signed to Lowsonford.
- **PARKING:** In a small layby on the lane near the canal.
- **LENGTH OF THE WALK:** $4^1/_2$ miles. Map: OS Landranger 151 Stratford-upon-Avon and surrounding area (GR 180677).

THE WALK

1. From the layby walk the few steps towards the canal. Just before the bridge gain access to the towing path through a gate on the left. Turn right to go under the road bridge and alongside the lock. A

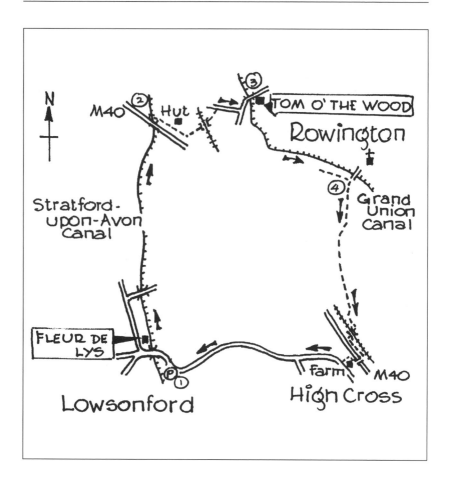

feature here is the barrel-roofed lock-keeper's cottage. Many theories have been suggested for the unusual shape but the one I give here is that the builder Josiah Clowes simply preferred to use and reflect the techniques of the bridge builders. Stay on the towing path for about 1¼ miles (passing the stanchions where the old rail route ran).

2. Go under the motorway bridge. At once take a signed path over a stile right. Go over a footbridge across a brook then climb another stile. The path is now alongside the right-hand motorway embankment. Pass a brick building and continue to climb a corner stile. Turn left. Walk at the edge of the field to a stile and tunnel

The lock-keeper's cottage on the Stratford canal.

under the railway. In a pasture bear left to a stile to a lane. Turn right. At a junction turn left to the Grand Union Canal and the Tom o' the Wood Inn. Just before the bridge over the canal go through a little gate on the right to the towing path.

3. Keep along the towing path with the water on the left for about a mile. Rowington (Roclintone in the Domesday survey of 1086) is over on your left. The village has a fine church which has much work (including the font) of the Norman masons. Go under the bridge numbered 62 then immediately turn right to climb the embankment to a stile to a vehicle way. Turn left to pass through the middle gate of three. This is signed as a public footpath and bridleway.

4. Walk along a clear track that goes through bridle gates to arable lands. Follow the tractor way alongside a left-hand hedge. In a far corner are two metal gates. Pass through the left-hand one and continue along a hedged track. Cross a brook and continue to a gate to a pasture. Keep ahead, climbing the rise by a left-hand hedge. In the top corner go left through a gate. Turn right to pass under the railway. Follow the way (used by cattle too!) over the motorway bridge. Turn right in the meadow to a gate in the far diagonal corner. Follow the fenced way to a lane. Turn right along the lane which goes back to Lowsonford.

PLACES OF INTEREST NEARBY

Seven miles east of Lowsonford is magnificent *Warwick Castle*, which played such an important part in English history. The castle is open daily and among the many interesting things to see are life-like waxwork figures in scenes from historic events. There are frequent displays in the courtyard. Allow several hours for this visit! Telephone: 01926 406600.

A mile from the centre of Warwick northwards along the A429 is *Guy's Cliff Mill* (telephone: 01926 492255). There is a pub in the mill building – a spot (where the Avon tumbles over a weir) that was loved by artists and writers including David Cox and Ruskin. From the mill the ruined mansion of Guy's Cliffe can be seen. It was in a cave in the high cliff near here that Guy of Warwick, a Saxon lord, hid in AD 929.

TAKE TO THE WATERS
AT DRAYCOTE

Draycote Water offers a relaxing and easy walk with constantly changing vistas across the water to the Warwickshire countryside, starting with the vantage point of Hensborough Hill.

Swans on the 'beach' of Draycote Water.

Draycote Water, unlike many reservoirs, was not formed by damming a river or valley. Instead, in 1970 water was pumped from the nearby River Leam to this storage pool constructed in open countryside. The huge expanse is about 2 miles in length and 1 mile wide at its broadest. See it in certain weather conditions and walking along the dams you could almost be walking along a seaside promenade! The capacity is 5,000 million gallons and when full Draycote Water covers 600 acres. The reservoir is owned by Severn Trent Water and serves several purposes. In winter, water is extracted from the river which helps to reduce the risk of flooding

43

in the valleys. At other seasons, water is allowed back into the river to give Leamington a reliable supply. More water is pumped along pipes to serve Rugby.

A country park covering 21 acres was created in 1972 by the County Council on the southern shores of the pool. Severn Trent Water Company has allowed the water to be used for an assortment of recreational purposes. There is a very active sailing club and fishing for trout is also very popular, both from the banks and from boats (which can be hired). To add to the seaside illusion there are names around the reservoir such as Biggin Bay, Musborough Shoal and Lin Croft Point. The circumference of the pool is 5 miles which makes an excellent walk. The admirable aim is to retain the countryside character of the area and your starting place is at Hensborough Hill, which is an excellent upland from which to view the expanse of water and surrounding landscape. Note: For health reasons there are restrictions regarding dogs – they cannot be taken around the reservoir, but are permitted in the country park.

There are very limited refreshment facilities at Draycote Water. Sweets and hot drinks and ices can be bought in the Fishery Lodge when it is open during the fishing season (approximately April to October). You will find plenty of benches and tables in the country park if you would like to bring a picnic.

The nearest pub is the Dun Cow at Dunchurch about 1½ miles away from the country park. The old coaching inn is open all day every day and has a good range of hot and cold food at very modest prices, including home-made soup. The pride of place must go to the pub's famous Beef and Bass Pie (Bass Ale has been used in the gravy!).

Telephone: 01788 810305.

- **HOW TO GET THERE:** The entrance to Draycote Water is about halfway between Southam and Rugby on the A426.
- **PARKING:** In the car park (fee paying) in the Country Park.
- **LENGTH OF THE WALK:** 5½ miles. Map: OS Landranger 151 Stratford-upon-Avon and surrounding area (GR 465692).

THE WALK

1. In the country park, walk over the grass directly away from the entrance barrier to the far boundary. Go through the kissing gate and climb the ridge of Hensborough Hill. The height of the hill

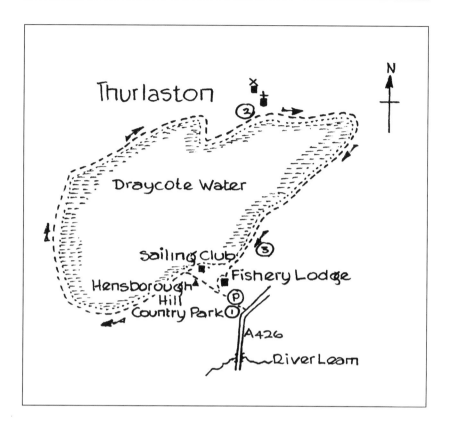

(where there is an Ordnance Survey triangulation plinth and telescope) is 370 feet above sea level. This is about 70 feet above the average water level in the pool. Enjoy the view, then pass the trig, plinth and telescope to drop down to a cinder path. Follow this to pass through a kissing gate. The sailing club is said to be one of the largest in the country with more than 1,000 members and 700 boats. Just try counting all the masts of the stored craft! Walk along the path to the vehicle way near the water. Keep the water on your right. Pass water installations and go along low dams. The grass around the water is all grazed by sheep, which avoids expensive grass cutting.

2. At the eastern end of the reservoir where sailing boats are prohibited is a favourite spot for fishermen. In 1998 almost 50,000 rainbow trout were introduced to the reservoir – sounds a lot but up

45

Count the masts!

to 400 anglers could well be trying to catch the fish at any one time! The hamlet of Thurlaston is on the hills above. (There is a tall brick windmill tower here.)

3. The vehicle way goes along the last dam called Farborough Bank to the jetties and Fishery Lodge. Go to the rear of the lodge to cross the vehicle way and pass through the kissing gate back to the country park. Turn left to retrace your steps to the start.

PLACES OF INTEREST NEARBY

About 10 miles north-east of Draycote Water is *Coombe Abbey and Country Park*. The Abbey dates from 1150 when it was founded by Cistercian monks. It was said to be the richest monastery in the county in the 13th century and is steeped in history. The Abbey is now the centrepiece of a splendid Country Park where there are plenty of walks and picnic places. Telephone: 01203 453720.

THE LAKES OF THE SPRING BROOK AT EARLSWOOD

Little could the builders of the third-of-a-mile dam of the Spring Brook in 1810 have realised the pleasure the lakes then created would give to lovers of quiet places almost 200 years later. There is a myriad of paths here to delight the walker, but one is rarely out of sight of the calming waters of Earlswood Lakes.

Earlswood reservoir.

A trite fact perhaps but canals need water – and a lot of it if the waterway is busy! With the Industrial Revolution many industries using the canals were centred around the Midlands. Unfortunately, Birmingham and the Black Country are on a high plateau which necessitated many locks – and therefore a plentiful water supply. The building of the Stratford-upon-Avon Canal was started by Josiah Clowes in 1783 and from the first, water shortage was a problem. To try to solve this, two valleys on Earlswood Common were surveyed.

After some haggling about £1,000 was paid to the Church in 1810 for a site for a reservoir. Part of the money raised was used to construct the local church of St Patrick. The waters of the little Spring Brook were dammed to create the lakes covering 50 acres. Little did the builders in the age of canals realise that almost 200 years later their creation would provide such a wonderful recreational facility. Beauty too – with a setting sun over the willow-fringed lakes and yachts skimming homewards the view looking west can be most beautiful.

Today (besides the boats from the sailing club which was formed in 1959) the banks are a favourite haunt of fishermen. There are many footpaths and bridleways around the lakes and nearby is the nature reserve of Clowes Wood where the silver birch trees are a delight in springtime. Earlswood (which was named after the Earl of Warwick when these lands were part of the vast Forest of Arden) is also a Site of Special Scientific Interest and wildfowl find the waters a popular gathering ground. This in turn attracts the 'twitchers', who a year or so ago spotted the rare Slavian grebe.

The pub on the route is The Reservoir. This is a Miller's Kitchen pub. Although therefore it is rather standard fare it is very good value. Special menus (and prices!) are available for children and Senior Citizens. The beers available are John Smith's and Courage with guest beers; Strongbow is the favourite cider. The pub is open all day from 11.30 am (Sunday 12 noon).

Telephone: 01564 702220.

- **HOW TO GET THERE:** From Birmingham go southwards along the A3400. Turn right along the B4102 to Earlswood (2$\frac{1}{2}$ miles).
- **PARKING:** In the car park just past the Reservoir Inn.
- **LENGTH OF THE WALK:** 3$\frac{1}{2}$ miles. Map: OS Landranger 139 Birmingham and the surrounding area (GR 116741).

THE WALK

1. Out of the car park turn left along the B4102 to pass the Reservoir Inn. Turn left at the crossroads. Within a few steps the road divides; take the left-hand fork to continue along the top of the dam holding back the waters of the reservoirs. Keep ahead at the road junction in the middle of the dam. At the end of the dam (where the roads meet again) there is the pump house. Alongside turn left through a kissing gate.

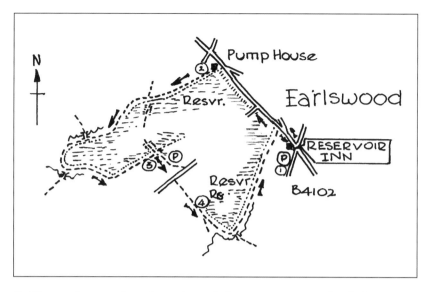

2. The path now has the edge of the reservoir on the left. We go over one bridge. Within ⅓ mile of footpath walking and just before a white metal bridge, take a bold path right which runs beside the canal feeder ditch then soon rejoins the waterside of the lake. Keep ahead at a bridge and junction of paths to go around the end of the lake. Bear left to keep at the borders of the lake to pass another bridge and a footpath junction. Herons can frequently be seen on the lake here.

3. At a crossroads of footpaths turn right. Go over a footbridge and pass through a kissing gate. Climb the winding path to walk past a car park and children's play area. (There is a good picnic site here with benches and tables.) Follow the vehicle way to a road. Cross the road and turn right. After about 150 yards and by the house numbered 94, turn left down a vehicle way which is signed as a footpath. The straight track leads to a bridge. Immediately after, bear left to pass through a gate along a signed path.

4. The path is along a low dam of the reservoir. At the end bear left (not ahead over the bridge) to again walk beside water. The winding track is through the trees with a feeder brook of the reservoir on the right. Keep ahead to emerge onto a road through a gate. Turn right to retrace your steps to the car park.

The pumphouse at the reservoir.

PLACES OF INTEREST NEARBY

At the village of Wythall 3 miles west of Earlswood Lakes is a fascinating transport museum. The *Midland Bus and Transport Museum* is open each weekend from 9 am to 7 pm. Telephone: 01564 826471.

THE RIVER ALNE AT HENLEY-IN-ARDEN

From the little market town of Henley-in-Arden this walk follows the slow-flowing, reed-fringed River Alne, passing a splendid old mill, and the lovely Stratford-upon-Avon Canal to the ancient village of Wootton Wawen.

The canal aqueduct at Wootton Wawen.

The pathways of this walk, beside a canal and a river, twist their way over lands which were once part of the great Forest of Arden where Shakespeare loved to roam. In *As You Like It* he tells us that here one 'finds tongues in trees, books in the running brooks, sermons in stones and good in everything.' Sadly, there is little evidence of the woodlands today. One of Arden's waterways, the River Alne makes a sinuous reed-fringed journey, recalling the marshlands of long ago, before joining the River Arrow, then the Avon. It is a waterway loved by waterfowl and you are almost certain to see a heron soaring slowly into the sky. The now lovely Stratford-upon-Avon Canal (completed in 1816) was in danger in the late 1950s of being officially abandoned; it was rescued from dereliction by enthusiasts and taken over by the National Trust in 1960 (today it is part of the British Waterways network).

The walk begins and ends at Henley-in-Arden, which is well worth exploring. This lovely market town has a mile-long High Street which contains a delicious amalgam of buildings displaying the vastly-different architectural styles over the centuries. The original market was over the River Alne at Beaudesert and was established during the reign of King Stephen by Thurstan de Montfort. It is sometimes thought that the first houses in Henley were built for market workers. The church of St John juts into the High Street and dates from the 15th century. The place of worship was built because the inhabitants found difficulty in crossing the marshy river to reach the older Norman church at Beaudesert – only a few hundred yards distant. Next to the church is the ancient Guildhall where folk from the town have gathered for 500 years.

There are numerous former coaching inns in the town but the pub I recommend is at Wootton Wawen – conveniently about half-way on the walk. The Bull's Head is a fine timber-framed building built in 1387. It has that homely feeling of inglenooks, huge beams and stone floors. There is a wonderful choice on the menu – the soup here is something special. There is an extensive wine list but the beers from Marstons and Banks are just right after a few miles' walking. The pub is open from 11 am to 11 pm.

Telephone: 01564 792511.

- **HOW TO GET THERE:** Henley-in-Arden is on the A3400 about 15 miles south of Birmingham.
- **PARKING:** There are several car parks signed in the town. Alternatively streetside parking is allowed.
- **LENGTH OF THE WALK:** 5½ miles. Map: OS Landranger 151 Stratford-upon-Avon and surrounding area (GR 152660).

THE WALK

1. Walk southwards along the A3400 towards Stratford. Go over the crossroads with the traffic lights. About ¼ mile further on, a path is

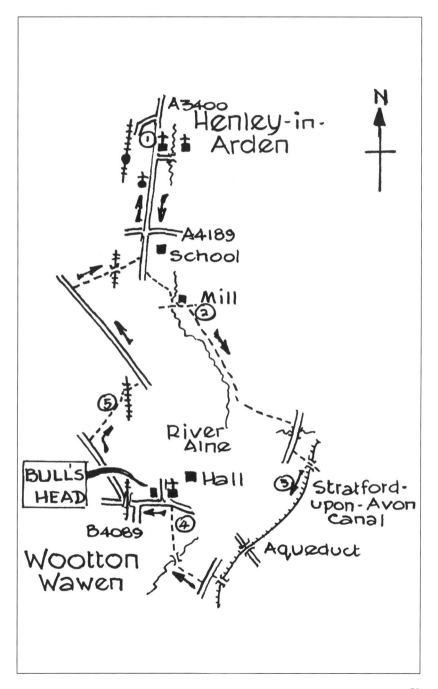

signed over a stile on the left. Cross a playing field to a step-stile in the opposite fence. Follow the clear path through scrubland to a bridge over the river. Continue to a vehicle drive. Turn left to pass by Blackford Mill, a reminder of the many mills once powered by the Alne. At the end of the cottages on the left turn right. The path is signed at the side of a field.

2. The path now is at the borders of fields, often running alongside the Alne. Over a stile by a little green metal gate the path enters a large pasture. Follow the arrowed direction; the path emerges on a lane to the left of tall trees. Turn right to cross a feeder brook of our river. Ignore a path signed down a farm drive on the left, but a few steps further turn left; the bridleway is signed down a wide track. The hedged way (perhaps an old 'green road') leads to canal bridge number 51. Turn right along the towing path so the water is on your left-hand side. A feature on the canal is the split bridge; this enabled the ropes from the towing horses to pass through without having to be unhitched.

3. Pass a holiday craft boatyard and go over the aqueduct which carries the waterway over the main road. About 400 yards further on (bridge 54) leave the canal. Turn right; the vehicle way passes bungalows to a lane. Turn left. Within 100 yards (by a metal gate) turn right over a stile. Walk alongside a right-hand fence to pass through a kissing gate. Continue to another then bear right to pass through a third gate. Proceed to a bridge over the River Alne (where I spotted the elusive kingfisher!). There are two paths signed – take the right-hand path now aiming towards Wootton Wawen church tower.

4. Continue to the A3400 opposite the lodge gate to Wootton Hall. Turn left along the road. Within 200 yards the main road bends right; keep ahead along the B4089 passing the Bull's Head Inn. After 300 yards the B4089 turns left by a toll gate cottage. Keep ahead to pass under the railway. At once turn right along Gorse Lane. Within almost $^1/_2$ mile and just past a white cottage take a signed path right. Climb a stile to a field and take the arrowed direction. Go over a bridge to the next field.

5. Walk beside the left-hand hedge. Over a stile turn right to a crossing place of the railway. Follow the clear path through a field then at the side of gardens to a road. Turn left and carry on for almost a mile. Just before the brow of a hill climb a stile on the right. Continue alongside a left-hand hedge. Climb a stile and keep ahead to pass through a metal gate by barns. Join a vehicle way which leads over a railway to the A3400. Henley is to the left.

PLACES OF INTEREST NEARBY
Ragley Hall is 10 miles south-west of Henley-in-Arden and set in a magnificent park. The 17th-century mansion with its fine Ionic portico has a large mural depicting the family of the Marquis of Hertford. The Hall and the magnificent gardens (designed by Capability Brown) with a modern adventure playground and nature trails are open to the public during the summer months. Telephone: 01789 762090.

STROLLING UP THE HATTON FLIGHT

The view looking up the 21 locks of the Hatton Flight on the Grand Union Canal was daunting to the commercial bargees of the past. It is still hard work for today's holiday sailors to take their craft up to the 330 ft plateau. Ramblers, however, have an easy stroll and can appreciate the splendid vista across the Avon valley to Warwick.

Lock-keeper's cottage on the Grand Union Canal.

The Grand Union Canal, a waterway of 140 miles from the Midlands to London, was formed in 1929 by the amalgamation of several canals; much of the route consisted of the former Grand Junction Canal which was opened in 1805. Early in the 1930s the government supported a scheme to rebuild the old canal including enlarging the locks to take larger vessels. The old narrow locks now used as overflow weirs can still be seen alongside the new locks. However, the scheme did not make the waterway commercially viable and trade decreased after the Second World War. Nowadays it is very popular for pleasure cruising and the tow paths are fine walkways and escape routes into the countryside. The section we cover was once the Birmingham and Warwick Canal and was completed in 1842; it includes the Hatton flight of locks which takes the craft down from the Birmingham plateau to the Avon valley. There are 21 locks over a distance of 2 miles and they lift and lower the craft about 150 feet.

Coming back you can visit the attractive church at Budbrooke, dedicated to St Michael. There is work of the Norman masons and many reminders of the now defunct army camp at nearby Hampton-on-the Hill (this was the garrison church for the Royal Warwickshire Regiment). When the Regiment left they gave the splendid weather vane to the church. There is also a monument to Rouland, Baron Dormer; strange really, as he was from a strongly Catholic local family. There is little else at Budbrooke except a farmstead or two – the map indicates that this is the site of a deserted village. There is, however, a fine view across the vale towards the tower of St Mary's church, Warwick and the battlements of the great castle.

The nearest pub on the walk is The Waterman at Hatton. It overlooks the canal and has some fine prints showing the waterway on the walls. Some depict the Duke of York reopening the locks after the constructional work of 1934. The pub is older than the exterior would have you believe – the building dates from the 16th century and was once called the New Inn. There is excellent 'pub grub' at the Waterman with especially good home-made soup; and have you tried a 'steakwich' (a massive snack) before? There is a terrace from which activity on the canal can be observed whilst sitting in the sunshine. The pub is open all day.
Telephone: 01926 492427.

- **HOW TO GET THERE:** Near the junction of the A4177 and A46 (Warwick by-pass) take the lane signed to Hampton on the Hill.
- **PARKING:** Just over the canal bridge is the free car park on the left.
- **LENGTH OF THE WALK:** 4 miles. Map: OS Landranger 151 Stratford-upon-Avon and surrounding area (GR 265655).

THE WALK

1. From the car park cross the water over the lock gates to the towing path and turn left. (There is a handrail but if you prefer, go

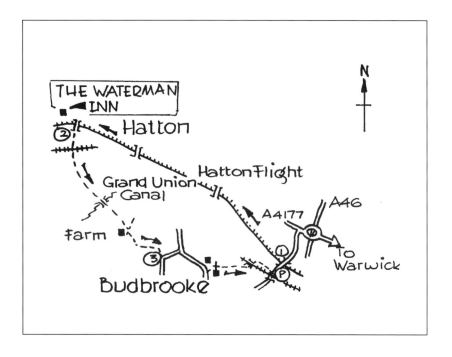

back to the road, turn right over the bridge and gain the tow path down the path on the left.) Follow the towing path to gradually climb the rise beside the locks of the Hatton Flight. At bridge number 54 (reached after about a mile) is a pool and British Waterways maintenance depot. Here leave the canal. Cross the water over the bridge then go down steps to a stile.

2. Follow the arrowed direction over the field then keep ahead to cross a railway line. Over the tracks take the indicated heading. (Note: there are signs here referring to Hatton Country World but these are right-of-way paths.) Keep the direction in the next field to drop down to a bridge over a brook. Climb the rise then make for a farmstead. Go over a stile by a metal gate then follow a right-hand hedge, then fence. Pass through another gate to a farm track. Turn right, then at once left to walk along the farm drive.

3. At a lane turn left, then right at a T-junction. This lane leads to the church at Budbrooke. Go through the churchyard keeping the building on your right, to a gate and stile to sheep pastures. Bear

The Hatton flight of locks.

right to cross the field to the fence stile. Go over the following field to the diagonal corner. Pass through a gate and under the railway. Turn right to keep at the edge of the field. Cross the brook over a bridge and continue to a lane. Turn left to return to the car park.

PLACES OF INTEREST NEARBY

Kenilworth Castle (5 miles north-west along the A46) is a magnificent castle ruin, parts of which are 800 years old. It was the inspiration for Sir Walter Scott's novel. In 1563 it was given by Queen Elizabeth to Robert Dudley, the Earl of Leicester and she came to visit on four occasions. The fortification was slighted (intentionally partially ruined) on the orders of Cromwell during the Civil War. The castle is open daily. Telephone: 01926 852078.

59

ALONG THE OXFORD CANAL
AT NAPTON

Unlike the boatmen of days long past we love the twisting and turning tow paths beside contour-hugging waterways like the Oxford Canal – not for us the straight and rather boring routes! Napton Hill crowned by its windmill and ancient church is never out of sight on the walk.

The locks below Napton Hill.

As with the railways there was great rivalry between the canals. Competition to get goods to their destination in a quicker time resulted in new waterways being constructed. The Oxford Canal to convey cargoes from the Midlands to London had the monopoly for only 25 years after 30 long years of construction. The link to the Thames was finalised in 1790; in 1805 the Grand Junction Canal was opened and the section of the Oxford Canal south of Napton lost much traffic to the new upstart. Today, after being in danger for a time of being abandoned in the 1950s, this is a beautiful waterway for leisure craft. Many know the busy Napton Junction where the Oxford Canal is linked to the Grand Union Canal. There are plenty of waterside inns, once frequented by bargees but now catering well for the holiday trade. The winding waters are also loved by wildfowl and herons are often seen.

The canal goes through the large area of Warwickshire called the Feldon. This is opposed to the northern Arden which was wooded and with poor soils. The Feldon is clay and is intensely farmed and houses were of stone rather than the sturdy timbers of the north. Always in the walk we have a view of a windmill. With its gleaming white sails it sits on the summit of the 500 foot Napton Hill. (Napton means 'village on the hilltop'.) Records of the mill go back to 1543. Not far away is the church of St Lawrence; the tower has been looking over the vale since the 18th century. The church dates from 600 years before and folklore tells why it is on the high land (from which seven counties can be seen) rather than by the populated village green – every night while it was being built the fairies moved the stones to the hilltop, so in the end the villagers gave in and built it there instead.

There are several pubs on the route; I think the situation of the Folly Pie Inn is the most attractive. It is alongside 'our' canal. The building is several hundred years old and was a popular pub for bargees until the severe decline of the commercial craft after the Second World War. It therefore closed down and became a farm until 1990. With the popularity of canal cruising it reopened as a pub specialising in beef pies. The beef is home-reared by the enterprising owner Tony Line. The beers are from the Warwickshire Beer Company and Hook Norton with excellent Strongbow cider. There is a fine spacious garden for those warm summer days. The pub is open daily with flexible hours.

Telephone: 01926 815185.

- **HOW TO GET THERE:** The start is at Napton on the Hill. Go 9 miles along the A425 east of Leamington Spa. Turn off right to the village.
- **PARKING:** On the roadside near the village green.
- **LENGTH OF THE WALK:** 4 miles. Map: OS Landranger 151 Stratford-upon-Avon and the surrounding area (GR 465611).

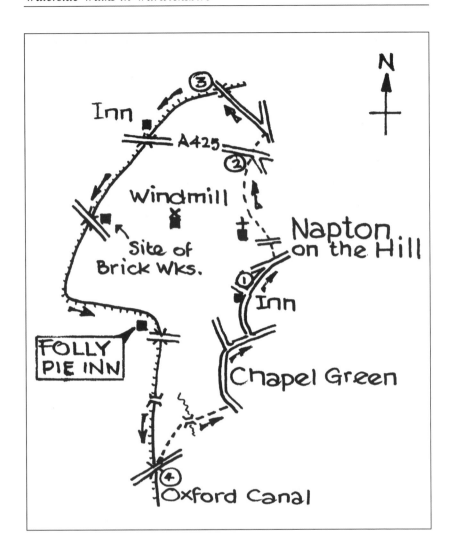

THE WALK

1. From the village green continue along High Street and Hackwell Street which climbs uphill. Just past School Hill (on the left) on the brow of a hill take an unsigned path. It is a tarmac way to the left of the cream-coloured Cardington House. At a vehicle way cross to the opposite clear path. The parish church is a few steps to the left. Continue ahead to pass through a kissing gate to a pasture. Keep the direction to go through another kissing gate and there is a third gate.

The Folly Pie Inn.

2. Descend to a gate to a main road and lane. Turn right along the main road. Within 75 yards cross the road. The path is signed through a metal gate alongside a new house. Bear right to a stepstile at the rear of a house. On a lane turn left to a canal bridge.

3. Over the water immediately go down steps left to the canal towing path. Turn right so the water is on your left-hand side. Pass under a main road bridge (inn nearby) and stay by the canal. Industries were attracted to the canal banks because of the easy transit of their goods. The chimneys of the cement works stand boldly in the countryside, and you pass, on the opposite side of the canal the old brickworks (the bricks were stamped with a windmill trade mark). The quarries where the clays were obtained have long been claimed by nature. In earlier times a large proportion of the villagers worked here and the works boasted they had the longest kiln in Europe.

By the first lock is the Folly Pie Inn. Keep along the towing path passing more locks to the bridge numbered 115. Here leave the waterway. Go up to the road and cross the bridge. A few steps along the lane turn left through a metal gate.

4. Take the signed direction to the right. Cross a bridge over a brook. Go up the rise then aim for the red roofed house. Climb a step stile to the right of the house. Follow the path through a yard to a road. Turn left. Follow the road through the village back to the green.

PLACES OF INTEREST NEARBY

Seven miles west of Napton on the Hill near Harbury is a splendid restored windmill. The circular *Chesterton Mill* was built (probably by Inigo Jones) for Sir Edward Peyto in 1632 on a wonderful site. The interior of the mill which is set above curved arches is open to the public occasionally (telephone Warwickshire County Council for dates: 01926 410410). Half a mile away on the Roman highway of the *Fosse Way* is a grassed area which was a Roman encampment. It covers eight acres and (as to my knowledge it has not been excavated) still holds the secrets of those far-off days.

WALK 14

A DRAGONFLY DELIGHT AT UFTON POOLS

✦✦✦

Small is beautiful in the Ufton Fields Nature Reserve. There are many little pools left from the extraction of limestone and pathways twist intriguing ways between them. You will be visiting Horseshoe Pool, Alder and Willow Pools, besides that delightful Dragonfly Pool.

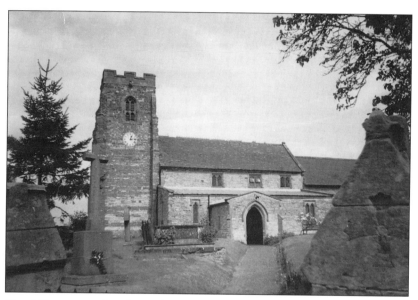

The 14th-century church at Ufton.

Mother Nature is so swift to restore the countryside to wild beauty after industrialisation. It was 30 or so years ago that the lands between Harbury and Ufton were taken from the farmer to quarry the white lias limestone for the manufacture of cement. When the cement firms sought pastures new in 1972 there were long ridges of spoil – waste rock and clay – and in between hollows of scarred soil. The 70 acre site was donated by Associated Portland Cement to Warwickshire County Council. They in turn leased it to the Warwickshire Wildlife Trust; the Trust (together with the assistance of local people) manage it today as the Ufton Fields Nature Reserve – a Site of Special Scientific Interest – for the enjoyment of all who seek quiet places.

The hollows soon filled with water after the cement company left and the marsh plants took root. Trees and bushes covered the ridges and grasses grew on the open areas of infertile lime-rich earth. Unusual flowers including five varieties of orchids can now be found, many of which have tempted the recorded 26 different species of butterfly to visit. But it is the dragonflies we seek on this ramble. There is a pool named after these insects, and allow time to settle in the Ashorne Hide to spot the six different coloured types. There is a nice contrast on the walk as the route also goes through woods of old-established trees such as oaks and ash, as well as glades of pine, alders and poplars planted in the 1960s.

The walk starts at the village of Ufton, on the top of a steep ridge, commanding fine views over the countryside. There is an excellent cafe by the roundabout which is open all day, but the village has a renowned pub on the hilltop near the 14th-century church. The White Hart was a coaching inn and no doubt many of the horses were changed here after tackling the steep incline. Earlier it had been a house accommodating the stonemasons building the church. This is a pub with an extensive menu so making a choice can be time consuming – but you can enjoy the magnificent views!

Telephone: 01926 612428.

- **HOW TO GET THERE:** Go along the A425 southwards from Leamington Spa and after 4 miles climb the hill to Ufton.
- **PARKING:** Park in one of the side roads off the main road.
- **LENGTH OF THE WALK:** 2^1/$_2$ miles. Map: OS Landranger 151 Stratford-upon-Avon and surrounding area (GR 379622).

THE WALK

1. From the roundabout in the centre of Ufton go along the A425 Southam Road to pass the cafe and garage. Just past the village hall the first footpath is signed down a vehicle way on the right. Keep ahead into a large field which is often under the plough. The path is alongside the right-hand hedge to climb a corner stile. The first part of the ramble is along the route of the Centenary Way. This long distance footpath was recently created to mark 100 years of local government in Warwickshire.

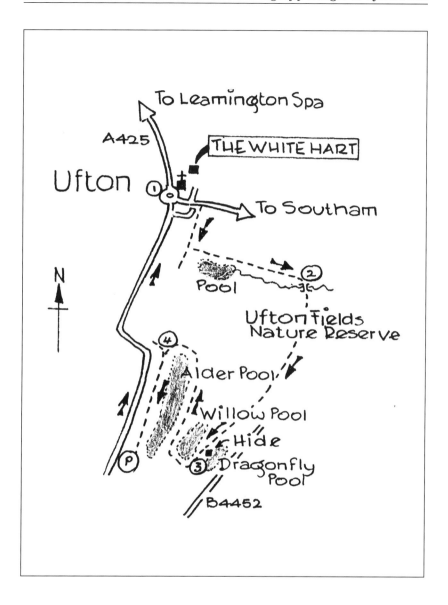

At the junction of ways take the left-hand path. The track is clear through the bushes with a pool full of wildlife on the right. A path of grass is reached; this is appropriately called Butterfly Clearing. A few steps further is a stile; nearby is a rusty wagon which was used to convey limestone.

2. Do not climb the stile but follow the path alongside the wire fence to the right. Pass over a little stream which rises on the nature reserve and feeds several of the pools. Keep ahead through a clearing where the old quarry railway once ran. Enter the woodlands and follow the winding path through the trees.

3. The path leads to the hide overlooking the reeded Dragonfly Pool. When you are ready, continue on the path through woodlands. There are several tracks leading off but stay on the main path. A welcome seat is soon reached; this overlooks the idyllic Little Grebe Pool. Then there is the Willow Pool where the trees dip low into the water and to the left as you skirt it is another delightful lake. This is Alder Pool. The alders line the bank and their cones attract little goldcrests. Follow the path around the pool to pass (on the right) Western Meadow.

4. Keep ahead at the junction of pathways. The path stays by the pool to a very informative notice board. Walk through a car park to a lane. Turn right and the lane will take you back to Ufton.

PLACES OF INTEREST NEARBY

Four miles north-west of Ufton is *Leamington Spa.* This place has been described in an old guide as the 'fairest town in Warwickshire and one of the finest in England for the calm dignity of its streets and the beauty of its gardens'. The first spa bath was built by William Abbots in 1786; since those times visitors have been taking the waters – and visiting the elegant shops!

WARWICKSHIRE'S WHITE RIVER AT ASTON CANTLOW

The River Alne wends a way through lush meadows near Aston Cantlow, where you discover a Shakespearian connection. The landscape is gentle and the village has that 'away from it all' feeling with no main highways disturbing the peace.

The Guild Hall, Aston Cantlow.

The river on this walk is the River Alne, the name coming from the Old English word meaning 'very white'. However, this is no foaming, fast waterway but a meanderer through meadows, its path marked by pollarded willow trees so typical of the English rural scene. The route follows each bank of the Alne and starts from the tranquil village of Aston Cantlow. No main roads pass through the place – but things might well have been so different.

The name of the village refers to the Cantilupes who were great landowners and lived here in a castle by the river. An ambitious member of the family, William, was able to obtain the much sought after privilege to hold a weekly market and annual fair. However, he underestimated the opposition upstream at Henley-in-Arden where the de Montforts were also entering the market business. The rival scooped the trade and prospered; Henley became an important town and Aston Cantlow remained a quiet backwater. The other family who might have brought bustle to Aston Cantlow were the Shakespeares. The parents of William Shakespeare were probably married in the village Norman church, there being no church in Mary Arden's home village of Wilmcote. There were no ecclesiastical records kept of weddings in the churches of those days so the facts cannot be verified – and Aston Cantlow is not visited by the crowds on the Shakespeare trail.

Although the place has sadly lost its village shop in recent times there is a splendid wisteria-clad pub near the church. The King's Head, where the parents of the Bard are said to have held the wedding breakfast, has recently changed landlords but will continue to provide good inn fare with the speciality Duck Suppers. At the end of the walk on a summer's day it is most pleasant to sit outside and watch the country world. The beers are Brew XI and Hook Norton but there are plenty of other brews for the connoisseur and there is the excellent Strongbow cider. The opening hours are flexible but include the usual pub hours.

Telephone: 01789 488242.

- **HOW TO GET THERE:** From the Wootton Wawen to Alcester road (B4089) take a signed lane to Aston Cantlow (a little over a mile from Wootton).
- **PARKING:** By the little green outside the pub or in the pub car park.
- **LENGTH OF THE WALK:** 4½ miles. Map: OS Landranger 151 Stratford-upon-Avon and surrounding area (GR 139599).

THE WALK

1. From the little green by the pub and Guild House walk along the main street. After 300 yards bear left along Chapel Lane. Keep ahead at the end to climb a stile. The Cantilupes' castle was nearby. In a pasture walk alongside the left-hand wire fence to a stile where the railway once ran. It was called by locals the 'Coffee Pot Line' because of the unusual funnel on the engines. Cross directly over

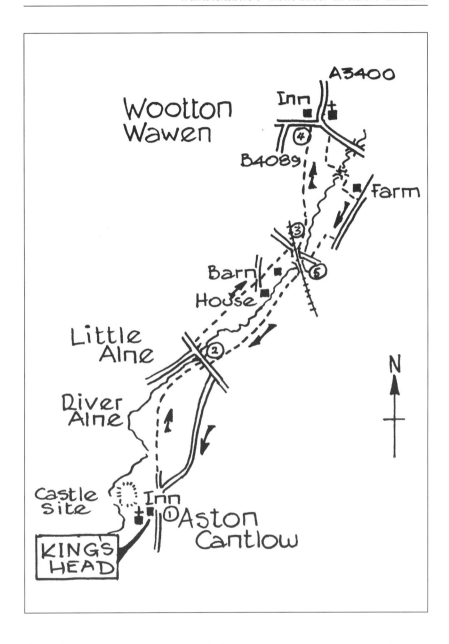

the rail route to the opposite field. Two paths are signed; take the right-hand arrowed direction to pick up the side of an old hedge and ditch. The river is now wending a willow-fringed way on your

The Saxon church at Wootton Wawen.

left. Go through a gate, then walk the length of the next field to a gate to a lane.

2. Turn left to cross the River Alne to a road junction. Continue ahead a few steps along the B4089. Climb a stile right. In sheep pastures take the indicated direction to continue to a ridge-top stile up the domed Round Hill. Descend, aiming for a point to the left of a farm. Go over a stile to a lane. Continue left, then at once take a path right. The path is over a stile to a meadow. Walk past a brick-built barn and stay on this heading to a lane. Go right to walk under a railway. (Here our river tumbles under the arches.)

3. Take a path over a stile on the left to go alongside the railway embankment. Within 30 yards is another stile. Cross a concrete vehicle way to take the indicated direction. Make for a point just to the right of a wired compound. Here you rejoin the river. Keep beside the wire to the end and climb a stile. Turn left (still by the wire) for 100 yards. At a waymark post turn 90 degrees right over the open field. Gradually walk towards the right-hand edge of the field to a new bridge and stile to a muddy field. Turn left and keep a constant heading through fields to an estate road. Continue to the B4089.

4. Turn right and ahead at the A3400. Opposite the entrance gates to Wootton Hall turn right down a cul-de-sac lane. Nearby is the magnificent Italianate-style mansion of 1637 and a fine tumbling waterfall. Go through a gate and keep ahead to pass through a kissing gate to a bumpy field. Follow the arrowed direction to a bridge over the river. Take the indicated way to go through a kissing gate to a rough pasture. Keep ahead through another kissing gate. Continue alongside an untidy farm to a stile to a lane. Turn right. After about $1/2$ mile and by the drive to Pennyford Mill, climb a stile to a pasture. Walk at the border to a corner by our river. Turn left to a lane.

5. Within a few steps take a signed path left to pass under the railway. Climb a stile to a meadow. Take the arrowed direction to gradually near the right-hand river. The path goes through a wood. Out of the trees in a pasture, maintain the direction to a stile. Go over a stream. Continue down the middle of a rough pasture to a far gate and stile to a farm vehicle way. Turn left to a wide track and then right to a lane. Cross to the opposite road which goes back to Aston Cantlow.

PLACES OF INTEREST NEARBY
Two miles east of Aston Cantlow is a magnificent *canal aqueduct* over the valley, a lane and a railway. It was in 1813 that the waterway was opened to carry coal southwards and limestone in the other direction. The aqueduct, high on its 13 brick piers, saved a costly detour or several locks. Climb to the canal from the lane to appreciate the great engineering feat.

WALK 16

SHAKESPEARE'S AVON

Shakespeare's Avon at Stratford was once a great commercial waterway. After its decline we have to thank dedicated volunteers and visionary enthusiasts for its rebirth as a pleasure route. The riverside pathways which once were used by horses to haul the barges are now very pleasant walking routes, taking you in the steps of the Bard.

The tramway bridge, Stratford-upon-Avon.

On this walk we wander (in poet Thomas Gray's words) 'where lucid Avon strayed'. The meandering river flows quietly through a green vale from the Bard's town of Stratford. Here he too would have walked (perhaps to drink at the Falcon Inn at 'Drunken' Bidford downstream on one of his renowned drinking contests). The route is part of a 9-mile continuous waymarked tranquil pathway beside the Avon to the hamlet of Marlcliff. During the summer months you will get many friendly waves from inland sailors – the Avon is a very popular waterway for holiday craft. The once busy commercial route was abandoned for some time before it was reopened a score or so years ago; some of the labour working on the Stratford locks was provided by guests of H.M. Prisons. There is also a myriad of water fowl to see, with many swans gliding by. Everywhere billowing willows dip low into the water and with the twisting nature of the river there are constantly changing views and points of interest, including some historic bridges. Early on the walk you have a splendid view of the Royal Shakespeare Theatre, which has mellowed with age since it was built to a controversial design in 1932 and now sits comfortably in the Stratford scene.

Nearing the end of the walk is a very convenient pub. The Old Tramway was built by a carrier, James Rudge, as a private house in 1857. In 1865 he obtained a licence for the house to become The Railway Inn with the horse-drawn railway running along his back garden. Today it is a comfortable Punch Tavern with many alcoves for that cosy discussion about the walk. There are prints on the walls to stimulate conversation. The bill of fare is not extensive but has all the pub favourites besides the 'Specials of the Day'. When I called there was the tasty Game Pie and I was almost tempted by the sweet called 'Death by White Chocolate with Lemon and Strawberry Sauce'! Vegetarian meals are on the menu – the Potato Dauphinoise could even satisfy a meat eater. The Old Tramway Inn is open from 12 noon to 3 pm and 6 pm to 11 pm but note – no meals are served on Sunday evening or Monday. It is open all day Saturday and Sunday.

Telephone: 01789 297593.

- **HOW TO GET THERE:** Stratford-upon-Avon is 25 miles south of Birmingham along the A3400.
- **PARKING:** There are many car parks in town. The multi-storey car park where the walk starts is opposite the Moat House Hotel.
- **LENGTH OF THE WALK:** $4^1/_2$ miles. Map: OS Landranger 151 Stratford-upon-Avon and surrounding area (GR 205551).

THE WALK

1. Out of the multi-storey car park turn right along the road with the hotel on your left-hand side. At a junction cross to pass through the wrought-iron gates almost opposite (to the left of the Shakespeare memorial). Follow the path to cross the river over the old tramway

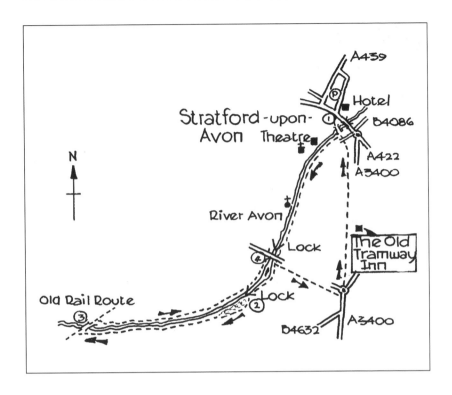

bridge. It once carried the horse-drawn carriages of the tramway which took goods and passengers to Moreton-in-Marsh. Nearby heavy traffic trundles over the 14 stone arches of the bridge built by Sir Hugh Clopton a century before Shakespeare's time.

Immediately over the water turn right so the rowing club clubhouse is still on your right-hand side. Join the riverbank and continue past the bandstand built in 1995 to commemorate the 50th anniversary of VE Day. You have good views of the Royal Shakespeare Theatre and of Holy Trinity church, where Shakespeare was buried in 1616, as you walk along the riverbank. Keep by the water to pass a lock and continue to go under a busy by-pass road. The road is on a bridge which once carried a railway. Follow the bankside to the next lock. Here we are directed to climb steps up a steep bank left.

2. At the top the path twists a way through a wood and you follow a well-walked route to emerge from the trees. The path continues at

The old railway bridge over the Avon.

the sides of arable and pastoral fields to reach that iron railway bridge ahead, then an embankment on the right. This wonderfully sombre cast iron bridge carried the steam railway on its route to the south-west. There are lighter vehicles today – it takes an enterprising cycleway over the river.

3. Within a few steps there is a tunnel under the old rail route. Here climb a stile and go up the bank to where the tracks were. Turn right to go over the bridge. At once descend to a picnic site and the river again. Turn left so the water is now on your right-hand side to the by-pass road.

4. Go under the road and immediately cross the river over the footbridge. Over the water turn right to again walk under the by-pass road. At once take a path left which follows alongside the road. At the end is a roundabout. Turn left to cross the road to a tarmac path. This was where the horse tramway ran. Within $1/3$ mile there is a way into the Old Tramway Inn. Keep on the path to the Butterfly Farm. Here go left to the tramway bridge to retrace your steps to the car park.

PLACES OF INTEREST NEARBY

Almost everything in Stratford-upon-Avon is, of course, 'Shakespeare'. If time is short or you have done enough walking there is a frequent bus service starting near the car park which will take you to the Shakespeare properties including the *Birthplace, Anne Hathaway's Cottage* and *Mary Arden's House.* However, for something different how about a guided tour of the *theatre* including the backstage area. This is an excellent introduction to the way the theatre works. These tours are Monday to Friday 1.30 pm and 5.30 pm (except matinee days) and approximately hourly from 12.30 pm on Sunday. Note however that last-minute changes may occur and you are advised to telephone (01789 412602) at least 24 hours in advance to book a tour.

WELLESBOURNE MILL AND
THE RIVER DENE

There were once many mills on the River Dene (a tributary of the Avon) and at least one remains at work. Wellesbourne Mill is a delight and a highlight of this walk which also visits two interesting villages, Wellesbourne and Walton, both on the banks of the Dene.

The watermill, Wellesbourne.

Although watermills were probably invented by the Greeks they were introduced into Britain by the Romans. However, it was not until several centuries had elapsed and into Saxon times that they were used on a large scale. The Domesday Survey of 1086 recorded that there were then 5,264 watermills and one could well have been that on the little River Dene near Wellesbourne. Mills were often the property of the lord of the manor; everyone had to bring their corn to the mill and payment was made for grinding it into flour. In later years with the ending of the feudal system watermills would be privately owned and payment made to the miller. It was the custom for the miller to also retain one sixteenth of the flour produced – sometimes the millers were tempted to keep more! The mill at Wellesbourne is open to the public and has been lovingly restored. The guide will explain the history of the building and the working of the mill. There is a fascinating display of country tools and memorabilia including an insight into the manufacture and use of coracles. Make time to visit the shop and see craftsmen at work, and a nature trail has also been laid out.

Wellesbourne itself was once two villages – with the suffixes Hastings and Mountford. The latter was clustered around Chestnut Square and you can note on the walk all the old shop fronts on the buildings which are now houses. Further upstream you pass through Walton. This is an estate village of 15 houses and included the school, farm, rectory, laundry and the essential forge – all part of the Hall, the seat of the Mordaunts from the time of Henry VIII.

There is a good choice of pubs in Wellesbourne including the King's Head near the church at the start or end of the walk. However, perhaps walkers would prefer the more humble thatched Stag's Head on the green where the floors are stone-flagged and boot-proof. The pub has been beautifully restored (approved by English Heritage) and sells a good array of beers including Boddington's and Marston's. The pub opens at 11.30 each weekday morning (12 noon Sunday). The food is good and well priced; a speciality at the Stag's Head is the home-made soup. There is a garden for those sunny summer days. There is bed and breakfast accommodation here.

Telephone: 01789 840266.

- **HOW TO GET THERE:** Wellesbourne is just off the A29, 6 miles south of Warwick.
- **PARKING:** On the roadside in Church Street near the church.
- **LENGTH OF THE WALK:** 4 miles. Map: OS Landranger 151 Stratford-upon-Avon and surrounding area (GR 278557).

THE WALK

1. Walk to the end of Church Street. Go through the gate to the churchyard. Continue to the left of the church alongside a brick wall. At the far end of the churchyard go through a blue gate. Follow the fenced path to a bridge over the River Dene. At once

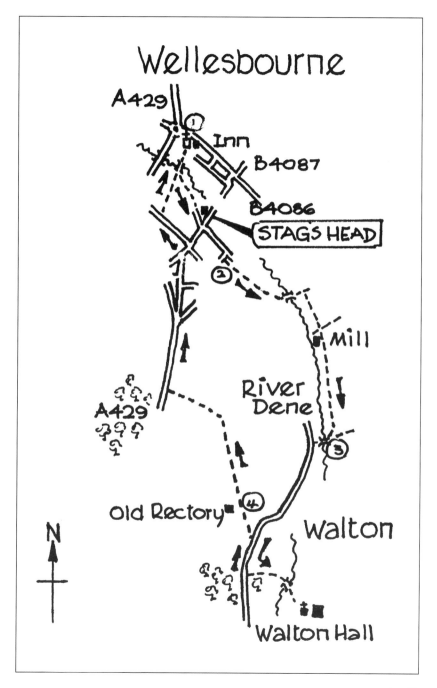

bear left along a path which borders the river. The path leads to a lane to the green. Here agricultural workers gathered in the 19th century to hear their leader Joseph Arch who was trying to form them into a trade union. Go over the main road by the Stag's Head Inn to continue along Chapel Street. After 300 yards turn right along Lowe's Lane.

2. Within a few steps turn left along a green track which is signed as a footpath. This becomes a winding path at the edges of fields. Go through a wooden kissing gate to a large pasture. Continue to a step stile at the far end. Walk 50 yards through the next field to cross a metal-railing bridge over the river Dene. Turn left to a corner stile. Do not climb this but turn right along the tractor way towards farm buildings. Go over a stile by a metal gate to a vehicle way. Here are the interesting mill buildings with entrance tickets obtainable at the barn, left. Continue the walk directly across the vehicle way. The wide path leads to a stile to a pasture. Further stiles show the way through meadows with the river on the right side.

3. The path leads to a farm track. Turn right to the picturesque ford. Go over the footbridge to a lane. Turn left to Walton. Follow the lane through the village with views of the great Hall. The Old Hall was greatly altered to the Gothic style by Sir Gilbert Scott in the middle of the 19th century. The redesigned garden included a lake formed by the damming of the River Dene and the magnificent Gog Bridge. The Hall was an army base during the war. It was subsequently a girls' boarding school, then a hotel, and now it houses time-share apartments with many sports facilities. The Mordaunt line had died out with the death of the wonderfully named Sir Osbert L'Estrange Mordaunt in 1934.

The road twists sharp left. By the second derestriction sign turn right along a house drive which is signed as a bridleway (but walk a few steps further if you wish to visit Gog Bridge, Walton church and the Hall).

4. Go past the house (the former rectory) and through a gate. Keep the direction. The track is soon hedged and leads to the A429. Turn right. Take care to a road junction. Turn right along the road signed to the village centre. Within $1/3$ mile turn left down Stratford Road. After 300 yards turn right down a signed footpath at the side of a garage. The path goes to the bridge over the river. Retrace your steps to Church Street.

PLACES OF INTEREST NEARBY

About 3 miles from Wellesbourne is a unique art gallery. It was established by Peter Moores in the wonderfully restored stately home of *Compton Verney*. It houses many modern masterpieces and is open during the summer months. Telephone: 01926 641777.

Near the centre of Wellesbourne is the old wartime *airfield*. Here many aircrew (especially from the Commonwealth) were trained on Wellington bombers. Although there is much activity in light commercial flying there is a small museum recalling the wartime days and several old aircraft (including a Vulcan bomber) are on display.

THE OXFORD CANAL AT WORMLEIGHTON

The engineers who built the delectable Oxford Canal were more concerned about saving costs with as few locks as possible than about distance covered on this twisting waterway. They therefore pushed the route westwards around Wormleighton Hill. Here in the quietest part of the county we can enjoy splendid isolation on this ramble from the delightful village of Wormleighton.

The Oxford Canal, Wormleighton.

When I walked this route beside the Oxford Canal, holiday sailors complained that they appeared to be going around in circles and getting nowhere. No doubt the old commercial bargees told the same story and added that profits were suffering because of the slow journey times. The reason is that the waterway was built as a contour canal; the route twisted around this hill, then that to maintain the water level and so obviate the need for unnecessary and expensive locks. The canal is almost 80 miles in length from Longford near Coventry to Oxford – perhaps double the direct distance. This was another of the routes planned by the great engineer James Brindley, who had his ideas accepted by Parliament in 1760. Its completion took almost 30 years, Brindley having died when only 16 miles had been dug. To reduce the journey time and distance (by 13 miles) many bends were eliminated on the northern section in about 1830. However (especially during warm summers with its popular use), water shortage has always been a problem. That said, for leisure cruisers and ramblers seeking quiet places this is a most tranquil waterway and goes deep into the lovely countryside – a real 'away from it all' treat.

There is no inn on the route; however, the Butcher's Arms at Priors Hardwick nearby is a country gem. Here 'ye olde pub' has been skilfully grafted onto a modern restaurant. This is no 'with chips' place but if you like exquisite food in delightful surroundings after your walk this is the place for you. Keg beers (no real ale) are sold but of course fine wines (especially Portuguese) are more in keeping with the meals! The pub is open every day but note it is closed Saturday lunchtime and Sunday evening.

Telephone: 01327 260504.

- **HOW TO GET THERE:** Going south from Leamington Spa take the A425 then the A423. Five miles along the B423 turn left to Wormleighton.
- **PARKING:** On the roadside in Wormleighton.
- **LENGTH OF THE WALK:** 4 miles. Map: OS Landranger 151 Stratford-upon-Avon and surrounding area (GR 449536).

THE WALK

1. From the stone bus shelter at the road junction go along the no through lane into the village of Wormleighton. At a green go through the Spencer gateway and walk to the left of the memorial tree to rejoin the lane. If you wonder about the tree planted in memory of Princess Diana, the answer is found on the fine stone arch dated 1613 which bears the Spencer coat of arms. The Spencers were Lords of the Manor (a manor which was moved uphill when the canal was built!) and in the 16th century Robert Spencer was said to be the richest man in England. There are memorials to the Spencers in the 13th-century Horton-stone church, but there are no

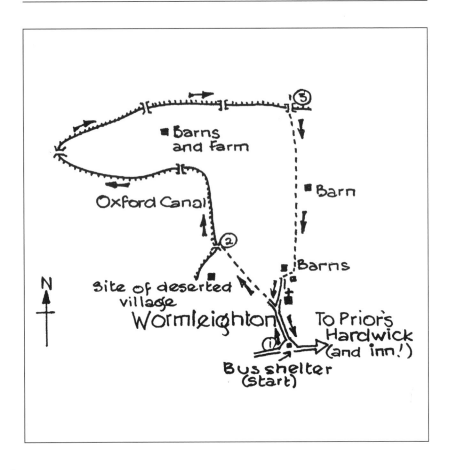

such obvious reminders of an even more illustrious family. The Washingtons were joined to the Spencers by marriage and the names are entered in the church registers as early as 1595.

Just before the church the lane divides. Take the left-hand fork to the end of the lane. Climb the stile to sheep pastures. Aim towards the bridge in the far diagonal corner (to the left is the site of the deserted medieval village).

2. Climb a corner stile and proceed over the canal bridge. At once go left to the towing path and turn left again to pass under the bridge. Walk with the canal on your right-hand side. Pass farmsteads and woods and go under bridges.

The gateway built for the Spencers in 1613.

3. Leave the water at bridge number 128. Climb the bank to a farm track. Turn right to go over the water and follow the tractor way. Climb the hill to turn right to pass a large Dutch barn. The farm track becomes a lane to go by lovely thatched cottages and Wormleighton church. Rejoin the outward route and retrace your steps towards the bus shelter.

PLACES OF INTEREST NEARBY

Four miles west of Wormleighton is *Burton Dassett Country Park*. These breezy hills were once extensively worked over many centuries for limestone; now sheep graze over the steep slopes. There is a large Norman church and little more except wonderful views – the village was depopulated in medieval times by Sir Edward Belknap who was Lord of the Manor. A few miles from the Country Park is *Edge Hill*. The uplands overlook the site (now on restricted Ministry of Defence land) of the opening skirmish in the Civil War in 1642. It was on Edge Hill that Charles I raised the Royalist standard before the great battle. A pub with spectacular views now stands on the historic spot.

WALK 19
AMBLING ALONG THE
AVON VALE FROM BIDFORD

It is difficult to imagine that Shakespeare must have gazed into the Avon (and loved the view to the old church) from the same bridge at Bidford as we do today. The waters still flow gently through reeded banks – and also still occasionally spill across the lush green meadows. The walk leaves the Avon to visit two other interesting villages, Barton and Marlcliff, with a weir and a garden to enjoy.

Bidford bridge over the Avon.

Until a few years ago the ancient commercial route along the River Avon from the sea and the Severn was not navigable. Through years of neglect the locks had become unworkable, the silt had built up and the reeds had encroached from the banks. A group of stalwarts worked hard to restore the route – often assisted by volunteers from the local prisons. Today this is one of the most popular waterways for the inland leisure sailor; there are unlimited possibilities now with the connections with the canal network at Stratford. One can understand its popularity for the river twists this way and that with a constantly changing vista of the English countryside and within each mile or so is an interesting or historic town or village. The bargees of old knew where to site a delightful waterside pub too!

One such interesting place is Bidford-on-Avon where this walk starts. It was Byda's Ford to the Saxons; here they could cross the shallow river. There are several pubs in Bidford and the Anglo Saxon is a reminder of the past – I remember a few years ago that a Saxon burial ground was unearthed when a car park was under construction. There is a fine inn at Barton where the frontage in summertime is festooned with flowers. Part of the route of this walk away from Bidford is along the 9-mile Avon Valley Path which hugs the riverbank downstream from Stratford. The Path goes to Barton where the waters tumble over a wide rocky weir – a very pretty spot.

The Cottage of Content is a free house which sells a good range of beers and lagers (the Becks was especially good!) The food menu is modest but wide enough to satisfy all tastes (including vegetarians). The salads and steak and kidney pie were especially good and tasted even better sitting outside on a summer's day! The pub is open each weekday from 11 am and the usual Sunday hours apply.

Telephone: 01789 772279.

- **HOW TO GET THERE:** Bidford is about halfway along the B439 road between Stratford-upon-Avon and Evesham.
- **PARKING:** In the car park by the recreation ground just over the bridge on the B4085.
- **LENGTH OF THE WALK:** 2½ miles. Map: OS Landranger 150 Worcester, the Malverns and surrounding area (GR 099517).

THE WALK

1. You might like to look at Bidford bridge before you begin. It is said Shakespeare must have passed this way when he visited the local hostelries during one of his renowned drinking contests. The Falcon (13th-century) still stands in the village but is no longer an inn and was where the Bard became very drunk; he slept off the effects under a crab apple tree. To this day there is a doggerel rhyme which refers to 'Drunken Bidford'.

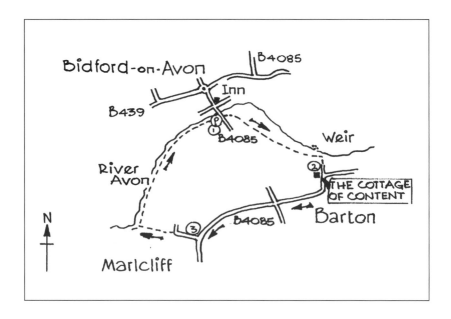

From the car park cross the road to a stile to a pasture. Bearing right walk over the grass, passing obsolete stiles. The river and the church are to the left. The path then goes through arable lands and continues to a flood protection bank. Go over a corner step stile and follow the track above the river walking alongside a wooden fence.

2. The path bears right to a gate to a cul de sac lane at Barton. Walk along this a few steps to the road by the pub, the Cottage of Content. Turn right to pass pretty cottages fronted by staddle stones which look like giant mushrooms (the stones were originally used to raise grain barns off the ground against the rats). Follow the road around the bend to crossroads. Go straight over and continue to Marlcliff.

3. As the road bends sharp left, turn right along a lane signed as a no through road. At the little green bear left along a stoney vehicle way that runs alongside a beautiful garden. You can see it from the path but sometimes it is open to the public. Just before a car park take a signed path over a stile right. In a large pasture the path runs alongside the river. The path is clear and leads to a recreation ground. Keep by the Avon back to the car park at Bidford.

A corner of Barton.

PLACES OF INTEREST NEARBY

Eight miles from Bidford is the old market town of *Evesham*. There are many interesting buildings including the ruins of the Abbey which was built originally in 1319 and then suffered under Henry VIII. The last Abbot built the still intact splendid Bell Tower. Nearby are two Norman churches, the stocks and the Almonry (now a museum and housing local antiquities and bygones). The site of the great Battle of Evesham (1265) when the rebels under Simon de Montfort were defeated is just to the north of the town and is on private land.

WALK 20

SHIPSTON AND THE
TRANQUIL STOUR

In its shallow, tranquil valley the Stour flows westwards before suddenly deciding north is the right way to link with the Avon. These were once sheeplands and though today the pathways are mainly through arable fields these remain quiet ways to pretty villages, including Barcheston with its surprising church tower.

The 300 year old bridge over the Stour.

There are at least five River Stours in England. The name comes from an Anglo-Saxon word meaning a 'strong, powerful waterway'. Not so the Warwickshire Stour – here the waters twist this way and that on a languid route before being swallowed by the Avon. This walk starts at the old 'sheep' town of Shipston, once one of the greatest wool markets in the kingdom. It was here that the sheep were washed in the river in early summer before being driven up to the Cotswold heights after lambing. Today it is no longer a market town but it has a fine olde worlde charm with many traditional shops (including, surprisingly in this day and age, three butchers). Several interesting villages nestle in our valley, including Barcheston. The tower of Barcheston church has leaned 20 inches out of the upright for many centuries. (Unlike that at Pisa this tower is stable with its present incline.) And it was at Barcheston's Manor House Farm that William Sheldon established his tapestry looms in 1561 after sending his son Ralph to Flanders to learn the trade and bring back weavers. The industry prospered until the popularity of paper hanging dealt its death blow. There is now only a handful of houses at Barcheston – after the Flemish weavers moved to a competitor at Mortlake and much later depopulation by cholera took place, the village declined.

There are many excellent pubs in Shipston but I like the Horseshoe just around the corner from the start in Church Street. This is a fine black and white 'herring-bone' building which welcomes ramblers who have worked up a thirst and appetite. The name would suggest a coaching inn and sure enough, for 300 years this was a busy stop on the posting road between Oxford and the Midlands. Although the road at the front is still quite busy there is a quiet garden behind the pub away from the noise. There is always a good selection of real ales (including John Smith's, Ruddles and Brew XI) and many imported beers. The meal selection is between traditional fare (steak and kidney pies especially good) and the more unusual 'specials of the day'. There are often offers to include wine with your meal. Visit on a Saturday and the Horseshoe is open all day. On weekdays the hours are 11 am to 3 pm and 7 pm to 11 pm. Sunday hours are the same but from 12 noon.

Telephone: 01608 663762.

- **HOW TO GET THERE:** Shipston-on-Stour is 12 miles south of Stratford-upon-Avon along the A3400.
- **PARKING:** There are several car parks in Shipston but the quietest and most convenient is alongside the bridge in Mill Street (B4035 Brailes road).
- **LENGTH OF THE WALK:** $4^1/_2$ miles. Map: OS Landranger 151 Stratford-upon-Avon and surrounding area (GR 260405).

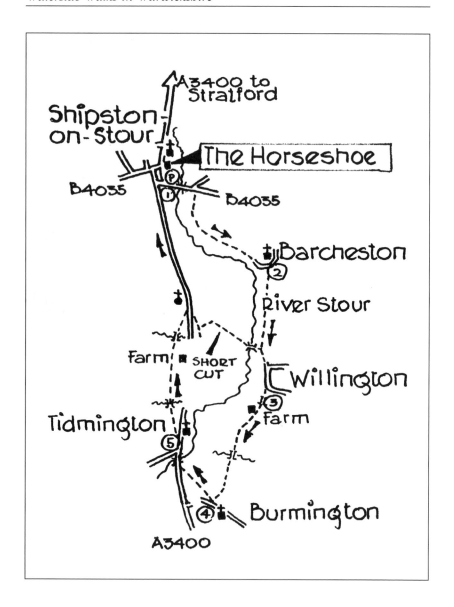

THE WALK

1. From the car park turn left on the B4035 to cross the river. The old bridge has carried traffic to Brailes for nearly 300 years. Within a few steps is a road junction and just beyond a path is signed over a stile on the right. The way is near the right-hand river to go over a

Shipston-on-Stour.

corner stile. Keep on the same heading to go over a double stile and brook which feeds our river. In the next field follow the line of overhead electricity wires to a stile in the far hedge with the twisting river still to the right. Climb a further stile – and note the old mill to the right. The Stour was once renowned for the number of mills its waters could support. Follow the path on a constant heading (with the leaning tower of Barcheston church to the left) to a far stile and a lane.

2. Turn left, then within 50 yards right over a stile by a metal gate to arable lands. There is a well walked path over the field to a stile and a signed meeting of three paths. Take the arrow direction ahead to still walk by the Stour. Here the river is faster-flowing and obviously a place loved by ducks. Head for and climb a distant stile. Walk along the path near the river to a metal gate by a tractor bridge. (For a short cut, you could cross the river and follow the bridleway to the A3400, which will take you back to Shipston). Through the metal gate, walk along a tarmac path. At a lane maintain the old direction to pass a stone cottage with its circular bread oven. Within 300 yards the lane twists sharp left. Maintain the heading along a well-used path to cross a brook.

3. Walk by a farm (mushroom-like staddle stones which once supported a barn can be seen nearby) to climb a signed stile. Walk by a pool (good for frog-spawn!) to a step stile to a pasture. Follow the arrowed direction alongside a right-hand wire fence to a stile a few yards from a far corner. Go along the next short path to a large ridge and furrow meadow. Take the indicated direction to a far step stile. Over this walk at the edge of a field to a gate to a lane. Turn left to visit the church at Burmington which was rebuilt in 1693 and the Manor House alongside which has work from the 13th century.

4. Retrace your steps along the lane to repass through the gate. In the field take the direction indicated for the left-hand path to the very far diagonal corner. Through a little gate climb the steps to the A3400. Turn right to again cross the Stour. Keep on the road past the tiny Tidmington church with its 13th-century tower. Opposite Tidmington Grange (about 400 years old) take a signed path.

5. In the large pasture turn right. Walk, never far from the right-hand main road, to a new step stile. Cross a dried-up gulley and go through bushes. Take the arrowed direction over an often sown field. Go past an electricity pole near the top of the field and by a corner of a field which sticks into our field. Climb a stile which is rather hidden in a corner by another electricity pole. Continue alongside a right-hand hedge. Keep ahead over further stiles and over a brook. Climb a field to a stile to the A3400. Turn left to return to Shipston-on-Stour.

PLACES OF INTEREST NEARBY
The *Wellington Museum* is at Moreton-in-Marsh some 7 miles from Shipston and is a fascinating little-known attraction. Moreton was a large training aerodrome for Wellington crews during the Second World War. The museum contains much interesting memorabilia of the period and is open daily. Telephone: 01608 650323.